FROM NAPA *with* LOVE

WHO TO KNOW, WHERE TO GO, AND WHAT NOT TO MISS

ALEXIS SWANSON TRAINA

ABRAMS IMAGE, NEW YORK

THIS BOOK IS LOVINGLY DEDICATED TO TREVOR, JOHNNY, DELPHINA, POPIE, TOTO, VERONICA, AND CLAIBORNE, WHO DEFINED AND INSPIRED THIS BEAUTIFUL LIFE.

Editor: David Cashion
Designer: Alyssa Warnock
Production Manager: Denise LaCongo

Library of Congress Control Number: 2017930311

ISBN: 978-1-4197-2674-3

Text copyright © 2017 Alexis Traina
For illustration and photography information, see credits on page 271

Printed and bound in the United States
10 9 8 7 6 5 4 3 2 1

Abrams Image books are available at special discounts when purchased in quantity for premiums and promotions as well as fundraising or educational use. Special editions can also be created to specification. For details, contact specialsales@abramsbooks.com or the address below.

ABRAMS The Art of Books
115 West 18th Street, New York, NY 10011
abramsbooks.com

CONTENTS

INTRODUCTION

Napa Valley is a majestic, twenty-six-mile kingdom tucked away in Northern California, with an exquisite beauty that gives any of the most visually arresting corners of the earth a run for their money. We all have different reasons for coming to Napa Valley: the light, air, soil, vistas, sunsets, farmers, architecture, local markets, wineries, hotels, restaurants, menus, naughty trysts, coffee counters, bakeries, culinary purveyors, healers, churches, back roads, back alleys, tiny shops, food trucks.

To me, Napa Valley is a tapestry of interwoven tribes of multigenerational families, farmers, winemakers, chefs, and creatives bound to one another by a common esprit de corps and the pursuit of magic. Magic in the vineyards, the bottle, the glass—on the table, plate, drawing board. Magic that punctuates many of our collective daily ceremonies and rituals that celebrate the everyday. It is this vibrant community of residents, weekenders, and summer folk who collaborate in and populate the Napa Valley I know and love—the bohemians, foodies, bon vivants, oenophiles, tastemakers, high rollers, and artists. Their creative fingerprints have enriched our homes, bookshelves, kitchen tables, bars, wine cellars, closets, and even our television sets.

From Napa with Love was inspired by a blog I wrote during my time at our winery, Swanson Vineyards, called *Alexis' Napa for the Curious + Eccentric*. I wanted to tell a fresh and different story about Napa Valley—one that illuminated a delicious world that was no longer exclusively a destination for wine lovers, but rather an inclusive haven of conviviality, hospitality, peacockery, stage setting, tastemaking, entertaining, hobnobbing, soul-seeking, and motoring. I touched upon ripe topics that brought to life the ceremonies and rituals that illustrate our passionate way of life, revealing an infectious underground aspect of Napa Valley that was both accessible and aspirational.

Alexis' Napa for the Curious + Eccentric scratched an itch that was still just a twitch. It catered to the visitors who traveled to Napa Valley to be inspired by a way of life; those eager to pack up the things they saw, did, and experienced and take them back home to Florida, Texas, Ohio, New York, or Fresno, for that matter. *From Napa with Love* is a love poem that takes the reader on an aspirational armchair tour of the valley as seen through the eyes of its most creative and intriguing personalities.

Introducing

THE
BON VIVANT

KEN FULK

with

JEAN-CHARLES BOISSET

*Ken Fulk is one of the great bon vivants of today, brimming with sparkly brightness, peacock haberdashery, and blinding talent. Ken is reinterpreting California design with a great deal of humor, nostalgia, and historic reference . . . and lots of fantasy. No one does a better gentlemen's bar, tricked-out poker den, English dining hall, or naughty boudoir better. Ken is, without question, a modern voice in the world of interiors, imagining design like an Old World theater director—where every detail is a rich, sensory experience telling a story.

ROGUES GALLERY TEE

KEN'S
Daily Uniform

RALPH LAUREN FLANNEL

DAD'S ARMY BELT

RRL BOOT-CUT JEANS

VINTAGE WELL-WORN ROPER BOOTS

* Whenever you see this icon, it is I, Alexis, the Authoress, offering my thoughts.

Why Napa?

We came to Napa in 1994 on our very first trip to California. It was part of a Christmas gift to my now husband, Kurt. We were living in Boston, struggling through the coldest winter on record. Dreaming of fairer weather and anxious to see what all the fuss was about, I heeded the call to "Go west, young man."

Needless to say, we were immediately smitten. We spent the first few days in San Francisco and then decided to head over the Golden Gate to explore Marin, eventually making our way up to Napa, where we had somehow secured a very hard-to-get lunch reservation at Tra Vigne. I can still remember what we ate—a garlicky Caesar salad atop a crispy flatbread, polenta with wild boar sauce, and a perfectly roasted chicken, all accompanied by copious amounts of delicious wine.

While San Francisco, with its jaw-dropping views and dramatic setting, was utterly intoxicating, it was also totally foreign. Napa, on the other hand, felt immediately familiar. The rolling hills and green valley floor reminded me of my native Virginia. Napa possesses a quiet, serene beauty that, to this day, still draws me back.

Less than a year after that first visit, we packed up and moved across the country to San Francisco. Nearly every weekend we headed up to Napa to discover new vineyards, shop for produce at roadside stands, and dream about one day having a spot of our own in the country. And within a few years, as fate would have it, we did buy a place in the valley. But rather than a quaint country getaway, it was large Federal-style house smack-dab in the historic center of Napa. This formerly sleepy village was experiencing the start of a renaissance, with artists and the like moving in and buying up the grand but neglected homes. Fortunately, Kurt's father was convinced by our unshakable belief that it was a good proposition and generously loaned us the money to purchase what was to be our very first house together.

We quickly set about restoring the structure ourselves, creating a kitchen where there was none and adding working baths where there had only been a water closet. During the process we also made an interesting discovery: thirty bottles of Prohibition-era wine carefully wrapped in newspaper of the day and stashed in a false bottom of an upstairs closet! Built in 1850, the house was one of the oldest homes in the valley and was originally located across the street from the Migliavacca Winery. Allegedly, during Prohibition, barrels of the contraband were rolled across the street when the nearby courthouse was closed for lunch, and then bottled in what was now our kitchen.

Eventually we found the bucolic setting for which we had so longed. Turning the handsome profit we made from our hard work on the historic house, we were able to secure an idyllic spot tucked into the hills above the valley floor. The seventy-six-acre property, marked by ancient oaks, rock-hewn streams, and a spring-fed pond, is a former cattle ranch now surrounded by vineyards, olive groves, and miles of white fencing. In honor of our first dog, we christened it "Durham Ranch." Little remains of the original ranch save for a 1940s cottage, which has been lovingly restored with a classic front porch (complete with rockers), an open-beamed ceiling, a stacked-stone fireplace, and board-and-batten walls.

More than a decade later, our Napa Valley ranch remains one of the last constants in our increasingly hectic and abundant lives.

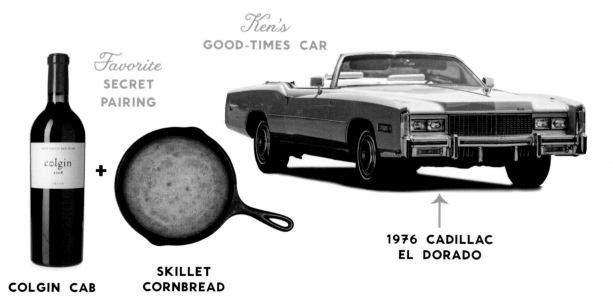

Ken's
GOOD-TIMES CAR

Favorite
SECRET
PAIRING

1976 CADILLAC
EL DORADO

COLGIN CAB   SKILLET
CORNBREAD

Q&A with Ken

WHAT IS YOUR BIRTH SIGN? Taurus

YOUR FAVORITE POSSESSION? We keep a framed poem in our kitchen at the ranch that was sent as a thank-you note from a dear friend after a weekend visit. To this day I still get teary-eyed when I read it. It ends with the line, "There are places that people shape; there are places that shape people." It pretty much sums up my feelings about Durham Ranch and the Napa Valley.

YOUR COVETED DINNER RESERVATION? A barstool at Press!

YOUR SIGNATURE GIFT Antiques

YOUR LAST MEAL? Spring pea soup with fresh mint to start, followed by homemade tagliatelle topped with shaved white truffles. For the main course, crispy roasted chicken with warm bread salad, and finally my grandmother's triple-layer coconut cake for dessert!

YOUR LAST SIP OF WINE? A glass of the premier vintage of Harlan Estate

IF YOU COULD HAVE DINNER WITH ONE NAPA VALLEY RESIDENT, WHO WOULD IT BE? The late Robert Mondavi

The Art of SETTING UP THE BAR

1 **SPACE**

Any public room should have a bar within easy reach. A bar can be a table or a room. It grows where it is planted. One of my early favorites: I converted a closet into a bar, covered the walls with fabric, and installed the shelves myself. It was the perfect dry bar.

I believe what makes a house
a home is derived from two
quintessential moments:

1. When you get the music to work
2. When the bar is finally set up

2 BARWARE—MIX IT UP

A bar offers so many entry points to good living—its many rituals and microcosms combine to bring life to a bar. A bar should be layered. Should be interesting. Should have history. And be saucy. It is the perfect conduit to become a collector; you can score endless treasures: trays, glassware, peculiar bar instruments, and tools of the trade. One gets choosier the longer one is at it, and the finds get better.

The Art of SETTING UP THE BAR

SILVER HUNT
CUPS

←

↖

COUPE

GLASSWARE

I love colored cut-crystal glasses—they are on the smallish side, not like some giant swimming pool of a drink. I've become obsessed with collecting coupes—I love to drink a cocktail or Champagne out of them, but not wine. Silver hunt cups feed my love for animalia—dog and hound ones, especially—but they are harder to find now. These cups are like a fantasy; they check all the boxes: silver, elaborate engraving, odd beast. It's a dandy in a glass.

4 PROVISIONS LIST

We stock clients' bars all the time and have our own proprietary list with all the essentials.

Favorite
BAR MUSIC
Blossom Dearie

**S
N
A
C
K
S**

SPICY PECANS

GOOD CHEESE
STRAWS

POTATO CHIPS + CAVIAR

GOOD VIRGINIA
PEANUTS

STOCK YOUR BAR WITH

TEQUILA • BOURBON • SCOTCH • RYE WHISKEY • GIN • VODKA • RUM • SWEET VERMOUTH
DRY VERMOUTH • CAMPARI • BITTERS • COINTREAU • FRESH CITRUS

SIGNATURE STAPLES

IT'S ALL ABOUT THE SPICY RIM

Favorite
COCKTAIL

THE SMOKEY JOE →

3 parts Tequila
1 part Cointreau
1 part Fresh Lime
A capful of Mescal

Add a spicy rim with equal parts salt, sugar, and cayenne.

Napa
SOUVENIR

Napa Valley Mustard Co. Brand's Hot Sweet Mustard

← *Favorite*
BEVERAGE GLASS

At the ranch we tend to serve our cocktails (and nonalcoholic drinks) in mason jars. They are hardy and hold plenty so that you can take one on a hike without fear of running out! For wine, we like the charm of a glass Dixie cup. It's utterly familiar yet totally unusual. Plus it has the perfect laid-back attitude for the country. Wine—no matter the vintage—is never precious in our household.

Ken's TREASURED RECIPE: PIMIENTO CHEESE

As a Southerner, I'm terribly fond of pimiento cheese. It's a staple of entertaining throughout the South. I've brought this tradition with me to California and love to have it in the fridge ready to go for the unexpected guest or midday sandwich!

Pimiento Cheese

1/3 cup mayonnaise

3 T cream cheese, at room temperature

2 t Worcestershire sauce

2 t fresh lemon juice or apple cider vinegar

1 1/2 t dried mustard

1 1/2 t hot sauce

1 t sugar

1/2 t kosher salt and 1/4 t freshly ground black pepper

2 T finely grated onion

1 (12-oz.) jar diced pimiento

8 oz coarsely shredded extra-sharp white Cheddar cheese

8 oz coarsely shredded sharp yellow Cheddar cheese

Tip!

TASTES EVEN BETTER DAY 2, 3, 4

A SOUTHERN STAPLE WE MAKE ONCE A WEEK IN THE SUMMER →

GREAT ON CELERY STICKS

AND GREAT ON RITZ CRACKERS

GO-TO DINNER PARTY

My favorite dinner party playlist is Amy Winehouse. For the country we use an assortment of Heath and vintage plates when dining indoors. For outdoors, John Derian's melamine plates are the best, featuring beautiful antique patterns. For the tabletop, I have a wonderful collection of brass candlesticks in varying heights. For flowers, I like to keep it simple, using ones straight from the garden—varieties like peonies, lilacs, garden roses.

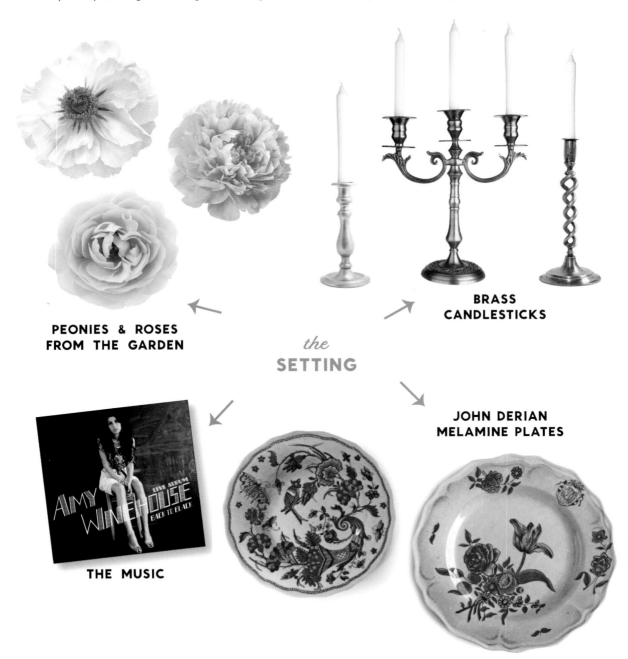

PEONIES & ROSES FROM THE GARDEN

BRASS CANDLESTICKS

the **SETTING**

THE MUSIC

JOHN DERIAN MELAMINE PLATES

the
FOOD & DRINK

**IT'S ALL ABOUT
THE MINI BOTTLE WITH
STRIPED STRAWS!**

WHITE CHILI

COCONUT CAKE

CORNBREAD

**(MY GRANDMOTHER'S
RECIPE)**

**MACAULEY
ZINFANDEL**   **PACIFICO**

Mr. Fulk's
FLOWER FACTORY

KEN'S FLOWERS
never
DISAPPOINT!

Ken is well known for a whole lot of things, but the signature touch of every dinner, lunch, coffee table, tablescape, bedside, celebration and installation is his extraordinary love for flowers and the loving gesture they convey.

Introducing

JEAN-CHARLES BOISSET

THE KING OF GUILTY PLEASURES

JEAN-CHARLES BOISSET

the BON VIVANT

Oozing with provocative and outlandish flair, Jean-Charles Boisset is a world-class bon vivant, alive and thriving in the Napa Valley, bursting with ideas and creation. JCB, as he's known to his friends, is a successful vintner who has incorporated his unique joie de vivre throughout his various wineries in California, culminating with his latest endeavor: the JCB Tasting Salon and Atelier Fine Foods in Yountville. Jean-Charles now lives in Bob and Margrit Mondavi's iconic home, Wappo Hill, with his wife, Gina Gallo, and their two daughters.

Jean-Charles is a shamelessly unapologetic one-of-a-kind living in a world of familiar richness and texture. He is an unusual mixture of intense creativity and business moxie—typically leaving others in a mesmerized spell, wanting more: more satin robes, more French accent, more red walls, more brooches, more fancy cheese and JCB wine, more Baccarat, more naughty accoutrements, more colored socks, more candles, and more leopard.

POCKET SQUARE

JEAN-CHARLES'S *Daily Uniform*

JCB COLLECTION CUFF LINKS

TOM FORD JACKET

RED SOCKS & LOUBOUTIN SHOES

25

Q&A with Jean-Charles

WHAT ARE YOUR FIVE SIGNATURE WARDROBE STAPLES?

1. I am forever adorned with my JCB Collection jewelry. creations of brooches and unique cuff links.
2. I am known for my many pairs of Louboutin shoes.
3. I always have two very unique jackets.
4. At home I enjoy three velvet robes with silk boxer shorts.
5. You will never see me without a pair of JCB red socks peeking from my pant leg.

YOUR FAVORITE RESTAURANT?

Our first love is always to entertain at home on Wappo Hill, but I also adore the food and atmosphere of Morimoto in Napa.

YOUR FAVORITE COFFEE SHOP?

Kelly's Filling Station in Yountville has the best lattés in wine country in the most unique gas station in all of California, and it is a wonderful Yountville community gathering spot.

YOUR FAVORITE COCKTAIL DESTINATION?

At Morimoto in Napa, where Eduardo and his team create impeccable cocktails with a great breadth of fresh ingredients and unique flavors, and of course, their amazing sake selection.

Love came at first sight of California and this incredible sense of place when I visited with my parents and grandparents when I was eleven years old. I discovered the land of possibilities, dynamism, and limitlessness. This was a powerful moment of creation with all these forces coming together—Spanish, Russian, American—going beyond everything that was possible then. Coup de foudre! Love at first sight! I was magnetized by California and fell in love with the incredible history of Napa, the heritage, the authenticity, and the freedom. I recall the moment I declared to my sister, "Wouldn't it be fun one day to make wine in California?" That dream was realized in 2003 with DeLoach Vineyards in the Russian River Valley, in 2009 with Raymond in the Napa Valley, and in 2011 when we finally brought Buena Vista Winery, California's first and most historic estate, into our family collection of wineries!

Jean-Charles's
GOOD-TIMES CAR

**SILVER 1979
ROLLS ROYCE
SHADOW II** →

One of the most charming ways to see the wine country is by train—and I adore the Napa Valley Wine Train for bringing that sense of Old World charm to traveling through the vineyards. The views are extraordinary and there is a great joy in traveling by train! At night, I'm inspired by the Napa Valley Performing Arts Center at the Lincoln Theater in Yountville. It brings fantastic art, performance, and culture into the heart of wine country, uniting the vital energy and artistry of performance and winemaking. I'd spend the evening with a world-class performance.

The Wine Train, with its fleet of beautifully restored Pullman dining cars, harkens back to the romantic era of rail travel and is all about a memorable experience. The Wine Train is touristy, but it is a must-do and one of the best ways to see the spectacular landscape of the Napa Valley while tasting local-favorite wines and enjoying course after course of yumminess. The three-hour train ride starts in the heart of the town of Napa and travels up valley, turning around north of Calistoga. Not to be missed are the daily winery tours, dining journeys, sunset rides, and the holiday Santa Train.

← **DINING CAR**

Tip!
**GET THE BEST
VIEW FROM
THE VISTA DOME!**
↓

FOR THE LOVE OF RED

Red Room, Raymond Vineyards.

THE IMPORTANCE
OF THE COLOR RED?

IT'S EVERYWHERE

Red happens to be my favorite color, as well as the color of wine. It's the color of depth, richness, fire, earth, dreams, and discoveries. We also incorporate the different textures of red—including red leather, red silk, red velvet, red corduroy, and even red shiny paint—into all our vineyards and tasting rooms to show the multiple facets of red wine.

The Red Room at Raymond is one of the most alluring rooms in all of Napa Valley because it was created from a blank canvas to be a tasting experience that integrates all the senses of red wines: from the rich red-velvet fabric and leopard carpets to lighting decorated with Baccarat crystal chandeliers and candlelight. It has been realized for the ultimate wine-tasting experience—animal feel, silk, velvet, softness, richness, power, intensity, energy, elegance, and vibration.

**BONDAGE
ACCOUTREMENTS,
JCB TASTING SALON**

. . . AND LEOPARD?

Because of their incredible agility, flexibility, precision, speed, elegance, refinement, and wildness. They represent a high sense of perception, intuition, and sense of nature. I love the leopard for its style, elegance, pattern, and its beauty.

JCB Tasting Salon, Yountville

ALSO EVERYWHERE

HOW DO YOU ENCOURAGE PEOPLE TO EXPERIENCE WINE?

Spontaneity is our guiding principle. It is encouraged by our audacity and curiosity. Our philosophy is to put our guests at the epicenter of the experience, experimenting with only inspirational guidelines. We are not here to tell them what they are supposed to feel. We want people to dream, engage, and discover while adventuring into the world of wine.

We believe people want an experience when they come to visit our wineries; an emotional moment that makes them connect to the wine world in such a way that they feel it as part of themselves. We want to create environments that share our deep connection to wine as inseparable from life itself, and to hopefully inspire people's passion for wine.

Favorite
SECRET PAIRING:
the JCB BUBBLE BATH

+

x24

I created the perfect recipe for a bubble bath that was dedicated to my wife, Gina: two cases of JCB No. 69 Crémant de Bourgogne rosé and the equivalent quantity of warm water. Gina and I had so much fun, so I thought we should do more bubble baths and share the best recipe in the world! It's exciting, original, and beyond it all, great for your skin.

"The best way to
VISIT NAPA
is to spend time together. Leave your phone behind and experience— to the fullest."

← *Favorite*
WINE GLASS

Baccarat's the Grand Bourgogne is my favorite wine glass. It has the perfect weight distribution, fabulous diameter, beautiful opening for the nose and the mouth. It's engaging and has personality!

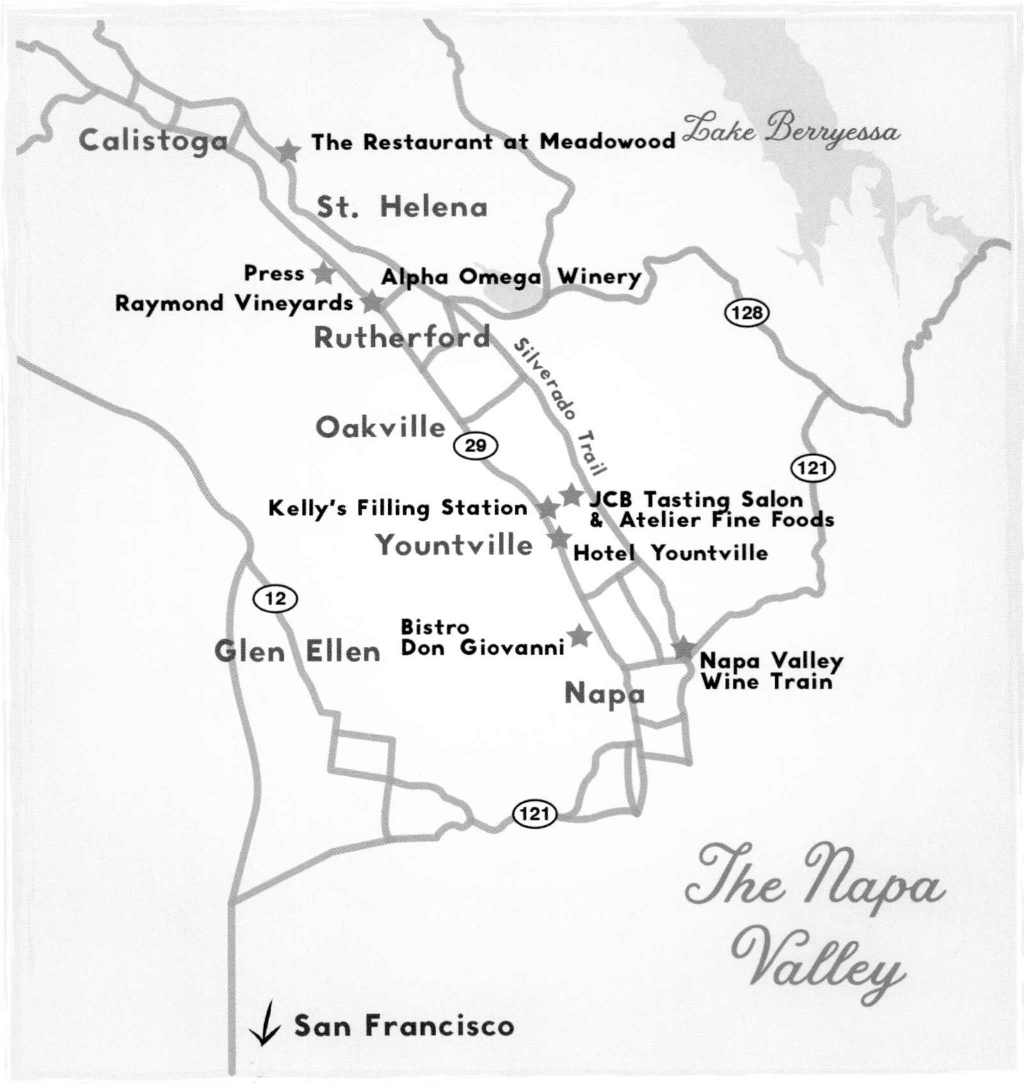

Calistoga

The Restaurant at Meadowood

Lake Berryessa

St. Helena

Press

Alpha Omega Winery

Raymond Vineyards

Rutherford

128

Silverado Trail

Oakville

29

121

Kelly's Filling Station

JCB Tasting Salon
& Atelier Fine Foods

Yountville

Hotel Yountville

12

Bistro
Don Giovanni

Glen Ellen

Napa Valley
Wine Train

Napa

121

↓ San Francisco

*The Napa
Valley*

Alexis's

BON VIVANT
GUIDE

WHERE TO STAY
WHERE TO EAT
WHERE TO WINE
and
MUSTN'T MISS

LODGING: HOTEL YOUNTVILLE

Looking like a spread out of the pages of *Metropolitan Home* magazine, Hotel Yountville has found its niche, catering to the well-traveled visitor looking for chic, cozy, romantic vibes. Guests are crazy about the well-appointed rooms with vaulted ceilings, fireplaces, and soaking tubs. I think their breakfast service happens to be the most yummy in the entire valley—and a priority destination for all breakfast lovers. Service is the name of the game here, followed by location. The hotel is within walking distance to all the restaurants in Yountville, and is ten minutes from downtown Napa and fifteen minutes from St. Helena.

Hotel Yountville
6462 Washington Street
Yountville, CA 94599
hotelyountville.com

Bistro Don Giovanni
4110 Howard Lane
Napa, CA 94558
bistrodongiovanni.com

Renowned for world-class food, Bistro Don Giovanni rocks year in and year out for many reasons. It is passionately Italian—the owner, the food, the clothing, the music, the flirty waiters, etc. They specialize in *delicious*—the pizza and homemade pastas are excellent. My favorite is the outdoor patio for a summer lunch or dinner, when they serve things like the Blondie Mary (made with yellow tomato juice); rustic gazpacho; fried olives; and pizza with figs, gorgonzola, and balsamic vinegar. Not to be missed is the "bostini" trifle—a 1,200-calorie extravaganza—or the old-fashioned butterscotch pudding.

Alpha Omega
1155 Mee Lane
St. Helena, CA 94574
aowinery.com

Alpha Omega winery on Highway 29, on the famed Rutherford Bench, is bustling all day long. It's always at the top of people's itinerary. Alpha Omega is only over a decade old, but it seems to have much more history. Two of the famous names behind the wine are Michel Rolland as consultant winemaker and Jean Hoefliger as winemaker. Their talents combine to produce lush, complex wines that can hold their own among any of the great bottles of the world. The chic, airy, barn-style winery can accommodate many guests and their various palates, offering something for everyone.

Cheese and all its naughty accoutrements are the backbone of every lingering afternoon, carrying into the night. In my opinion, Atelier Fine Foods runs the best cheese program in Napa Valley. It carries the most perfect and edited assortments of cheeses, caviars, prosciuttos, salamis, crackers, grissini, jellies, and spreads. It is a dreamy resource.

Atelier Fine Foods
6505 Washington Street
Yountville, CA 94599
atelierfinefoods.com

ELIZABETH
SWANSON

Introducing

THE BOHEMIAN

ELIZABETH SWANSON

with

IRA YEAGER

ELIZABETH SWANSON

Elizabeth Swanson is my mother, muse, and the Wizardess of Oz here in Oakville. Ever since I was a little girl, any time I walked into a 7-Eleven, hardware store, fancy party, or airplane, "it" always happened . . . a stranger would immediately race up to me with wild enthusiasm and animated eyes and say, "Are you . . . ???" Knowing immediately where this was going, I would say, "Yes, I am! She is my mother," all the while trying to piece together which part of her life this person was from.

Raised in New Orleans by a Cuban mother and a Southern father, Elizabeth is known for her magnificent joie de vivre, infectious humor, powerful jazz hands, otherworldly evenings and dinners, late-night tap shoe collection, magical wordsmithing, love of junk food and 1940s French music, red rubber boots, and most important, her kind ways. She is my family's everything.

My mother is the true inspiration for this book.

STRAW HAT

TUXEDO SHIRT

RUBBER BOOTS

ELIZABETH'S *Daily Uniform*

CRUISER BIKE

THANK YOU
FOR
VISITING

Why Napa?

I landed screaming, yelling, and in a therapist's chair three times a week. The idea of leaving porpoises, manatees, and the snow-white beaches of Florida for a dust bowl in California was beyond menopausal.

The truth is, Napa found me—it messed with my heart, taught my fingers how to paint and my soul how to sing over the roosters and chickens in my backyard. My favorite teachers have been my extraordinary husband, Clarke, and three daughters, Alexis, Veronica, and Claiborne; our Spanish nurse, Maria; the inspiring farmers who work in our vineyards; and my beloved goats, sheep, donkeys, dogs, and cats. They've reinforced my sense of humor and dedication to this sacred piece of land and valley.

Thirty years later, I am still landing and perfecting my pepper jelly, my homemade tomato sauce, and persuading gardenias to bloom in the garden. My cats are the real stewards of the property. God bless America.

Elizabeth's GOOD-TIMES CAR

SILVER 1966 MERCEDES 300 SL CONVERTIBLE

The Art of
THE TABLE
SETTING

If table setting were a love language, this would certainly be my mother's. Her beautifully festive breakfast, lunch, and dinner tables are works of art, imprinted by her loving hands and almost childlike eye, covered in trinkets, treasures, and objets d'art, which always tell a complete and magical story about a person, occasion, or celebration.

1 CREATE A TREASURE
TROVE OF KNICKKNACKS,
TOYS, ACCOUTREMENTS . . .
YOUR
Fairy Dust

ANIMAL CRACKERS

FRENCH RIBBONS

**STRIPED
PAPER STRAWS**

LOLLIPOPS

**PARTY
HATS**

**OLD COLLECTION OF
PORTHAULT DINNER
AND COCKTAIL NAPKINS**

**TRINKETS, TOYS,
PORCELAINS**

CONFETTI

2 CREATE A *Prop Closet*

Find a closet, drawer, or trunk to safely keep all your special props in (e.g., tablecloths, napkins, napkin rings, flower containers, candles, and votives, etc.).

Elizabeth's Secret Sauce
HER PROP CLOSET

🕮 A HOSTESS'S ULTIMATE PARTY RESOURCE

A prop closet dedicated to party giving is all sorts of magic. When surveying shelves of lovingly organized accoutrements, one's imagination is free to jump from weekend brunch to afternoon tea to dinner party to midsummer night's feast—in a split second. For the madame of ceremonies, the prop closet can spellbind/haunt/be a source of pride, envy, and admiration. On a practical and equally important note, having party gear arranged in an orderly fashion means you're set to have guests at a moment's notice.

3

FLOWERS, FLOWERS, *and more* FLOWERS

 **4** LOCATION, *Location*

To make special occasions even more special, I like moving the dining table to unexpected locations: in front of the fireplace in the living room, under a tree, in the barn, or in the middle of a vineyard.

WHERE IS YOUR FAVORITE PLACE TO ENTERTAIN?

Our 1904 utility barn, which looks like Marie Antoinette's poor sister's ballroom, and used to house animals and farm equipment and hay, is my favorite entertaining spot. The barn itself is so truly humble and architecturally perfect, with its old cement floor and tin siding and roof. Attached to the bar is our henhouse—so there is definitely a special perfume. We've had some of our best celebrations in there: dress rehearsals, Christmas masses, big birthday celebrations. Every night is different—sometimes the walls and beams are covered in corn stalks; sometimes it hosts the artist and my best friend Ira Yeager's newest oversize installations; and sometimes, there are just long tables and hundreds of votives.

My
BALLROOM

ENTERTAINING ESSENTIALS *at a* MOMENT'S NOTICE

MUSIC

Go-To
HORS D'OEUVRE

HOMEMADE
PEPPER JELLY

+

GOAT
CHEESE

+

TERRY'S HOMEMADE
FOCACCIA

GLASS
DIXIE
CUPS

HOMEGROWN FIGS

Signature Gift

For the person who has everything

EGGS FROM MY CHICKEN COOP!

Everyone has some type of intoxicating entertaining diversion at their home—the kind that brings out the inner kid/rock star/daredevil/badass in people. Some people have a karaoke machine; others have a high striker, or a mechanical bull . . . My mother has a collection of tap shoes for late-night revelry. Yes, tap shoes. At first the collection started with traditional black patent-leather tap shoes and then exponentially grew to include tap shoes in every size and shape, procured from the local Salvation Army and Goodwill. Someone's discarded loafers or Mary Janes were suddenly given a new life at the cobbler, with affixed metal taps on the bottom of the soles and colored French ribbons as laces. She has tap shoes for everybody, at all of her parties—and people can't get enough of these shoes, and their sudden dancing talents.

Introducing
IRA YEAGER
THE ARTIST

Ira Yeager is a world-famous painter above all things, and almost equally famous as a bohemian/raconteur/ entertainer from Northern California (mainly Calistoga), acting as though he were living in the eighteenth century. Ira is my mom's best friend and the wildest eccentric I know. With a mad mane of hair covered in flecks of paint and a permanently raised Dali-esque brow, he is always sharing exotic tales from every corner of the earth.

Truth be told, Ira is one of Napa Valley's great treasures and talents—his art is always found in the most interesting, eclectic, and photographed homes of Napa. Over the years he has painted everything, including magnificent Wappo Native Americans, Victorian shoes, Marie Antoinette's peasants, porcelain teapots, and Napa Valley landscapes. His work is often signed with the moniker "von Yeager, 1786." Ira's paintings illuminate all the humor, mischief, and ridiculousness of eighteenth-century agrarian life, as he imagines it. Life with Ira is always about a very exaggerated wink.

A BERET OR COWBOY HAT

A TATTERED TURNBULL + ASSER SHIRT

NATIVE AMERICAN CLOTHING

IRA'S *Daily Uniform*

AN ARRAY OF FANCIFUL STOCKINGS

BROOKS BROTHERS SHORTS

PAINT-SPLATTERED SHOES
(250 pairs and only one that fits)

Ira is famously known for **HIS NATIVE AMERICAN SERIES**

Why Calistoga?

Because it was the poor side of the tracks. We'd tell everyone we lived in St. Helena, but now that Calistoga is cool, I say Calistoga, not St. Helena. My city friends had started buying in the valley and persuaded me to come up. In 1975, I bought an old cabin, put a cupola on the top, and called it the Tucker Farm Schoolhouse to make it sound legit-ish.

My fantasy was to be a country gentleman farmer with my three grapevines and art. Since the seventies, I have purchased eleven properties; most of them are in Calistoga/Napa County. I paid no more than $80,000 for each of them.

HOW WOULD YOU DESCRIBE YOUR ART?

Basically, I am an abstract expressionist. In the 1950s, I attended the San Francisco Art Institute, as well as California Guild of Arts and Crafts (now called the California College of the Arts), where I was a student of Richard Diebenkorn and Elmer Bischoff and Nathan Oliveira—and friends with Joan Brown and Jay DeFeo. I was formally trained, but I have a very complicated psyche that allows my work to be multifaceted and very playful.

Being intuitive, I am always one step ahead of the trend. I once painted a series of teapots and everybody thought, "What a stupid thing to do," and then in two years everything was teapots. Most artists end their lives in a formula; I keep experimenting and continue growing and learning. Most artists use slide projectors to do their images on their canvases; I do all my own drawings.

PAINT-SPLATTERED SHOES

IRA'S HOBBY *and* SIGNATURE GIFT

PORTRAITS ON JACKETS →

I like to collect old vests and jackets and add bits of things to them: Navajo buttons, beadwork, silver tips, silver moons, and clouds. On the back of the vest or jacket, I'll paint a Native American portrait.

ENTERTAINING ESSENTIALS *at a* MOMENT'S NOTICE

**EIGHTEENTH-CENTURY
COLORED CUT CRYSTAL**

+

**BLACK
BOX
RED WINE**

JOHNNY CASH

JUKEBOX
Depending on the mood and
subject: Sometimes I listen to
Alice Cooper on Pandora;
other times esoteric eighteenth-
century music. And I love music
Americana.

Ira's Go-To
HORS D'OEUVRE

+

**MY FAMOUS
CHEEZ-IT RECIPE**

Cheez-It Hors D'oeuvre*

1. Flash soak Cheez-Its
   in ice water
2. Pat dry with
   paper towels
3. Cover in butter
4. Bake at 275°F
   until crispy

 ***Serve at your own risk**

HOW DO YOU WORK AND LIVE?

Like Fidel Castro did, I moved around night to night because I like the different energies of each house. When you work as much as I do, you need the different inspirations and atmospheres. There's the Swedish villa; the rickety horse barn in Sonoma County that I converted into a French hunting lodge from the 1800s with horse-stall bedrooms and Parisian spiral staircase that was a gift from Maurice Chevalier's niece; the Treehouse; Palazzetto Cervo; and Villa du Lac, an eighteenth-century Italian-style lake house just outside of Napa on Hidden Valley Lake, which reminds me of Venice because no motorboats are allowed on the water.

Then there is my Winter Palace (for the summer) and the Summer Palace (for the winter). The big parties go on at the Arcanum Priory in the Sea Ranch. (Translation: The jail where the geniuses who know how to make gold are locked away.) Naughty parties are held in the Green Barn with all the Italians from Castello di Amorosa.

"*I always wanted to be*
AN ARTIST,
of course. I wanted to be a Bohemian living in NYC's Greenwich Village, wearing black, having candles in wine bottles dripping in wax, and drinking red wine."

Q&A with Ira

WHAT IS YOUR FAVORITE CALISTOGA HOTEL?

Calistoga Inn because it is the most approachable. There
aren't many rooms and it is kind of down home.

WHAT IS YOUR FAVORITE CALISTOGA RESTAURANT? WHAT DO YOU
ORDER THERE?

Soo Yuan. I order the Ginger Chicken. It is the best-kept
secret in Calistoga. Carol the owner is a good friend.

IF YOU HAD FRIENDS IN TOWN, WHAT IS THE ONE THING NOT
TO BE MISSED?

The Napa Valley Reserve and the Auberge du Soleil. I even
had them order me a waiter vest that I wear there, that
I embellished with silver moons and thunder clouds, so I
can be confused with the waiters.

WHAT IS YOUR FAVORITE WATERING HOLE?

Solbar.

WHAT IS YOUR FAVORITE SATURDAY AFTERNOON NAPA EXCURSION?

To the coast-I love the drive on Highway 1. I buy a lot
of treasures at my three favorite antiques shops in
Guerneville. I am also a regular at the Guerneville Flea
Market, where I bought a Walter Keane painting. Lunch is
at the taco truck at the Cal Mart parking lot.

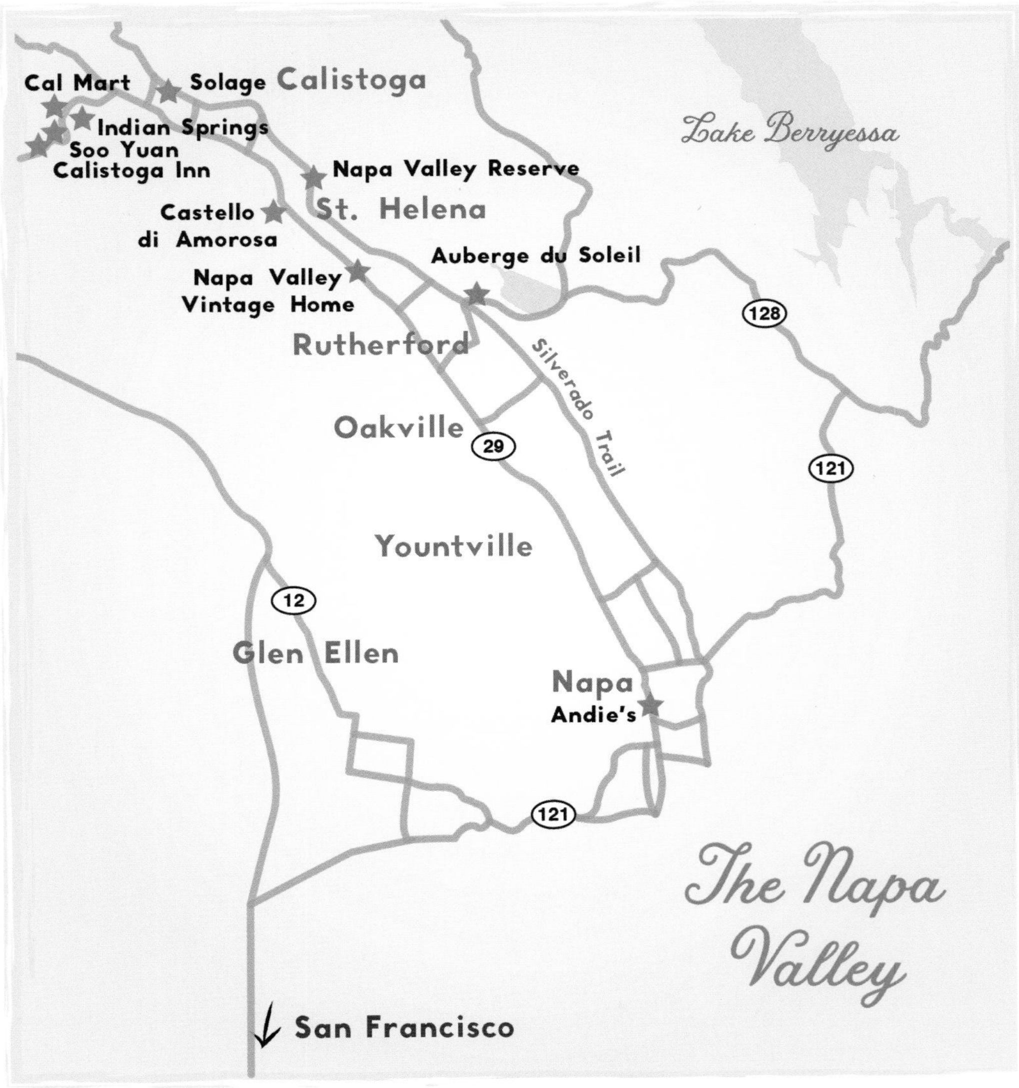

Cal Mart ⭐ ⭐ Solage **Calistoga**
⭐
⭐ Indian Springs
Soo Yuan
Calistoga Inn ⭐ Napa Valley Reserve

St. Helena

Castello ⭐
di Amorosa

Auberge du Soleil
Napa Valley ⭐
Vintage Home ⭐

Rutherford

Oakville 29

Yountville

12

Glen Ellen

Napa
Andie's ⭐

Lake Berryessa

128

121

121

The Napa
Valley

Silverado Trail

↓ **San Francisco**

Alexis's

BOHEMIAN
GUIDE

WHERE TO STAY
WHERE TO EAT
WHERE TO WINE
and
MUSTN'T MISS

LODGING: INDIAN SPRINGS

Indian Springs Resort and Spa, nestled at the farthest end of Napa Valley, is one of the more charming and nostalgic relics standing. It's a time capsule and healing refuge, where the spirit of California is alive and well at their historic spa, in the form of real-deal 100% pure volcanic ash mud baths—an experience and procedure that hasn't changed in over a hundred years. Everything about Indian Springs has a vintage feel about it, including the menu of services, facilities, architecture, landscape, accommodations, and amusements. There is an undeniable sense that you have stumbled upon a very well-kept secret upon arrival.

My own love affair with Indian Springs began one early February morning many years ago, when an out-of-town friend was staying at the hotel and invited me and my bathing suit over for a swim. I drove up and was immediately enchanted by a world frozen in the 1930s. The property is enveloped by palm trees and is dotted with white cottages with brightly painted doors and front porches. Four geysers on the property dramatically pump steam plumes. It is the sort of place where people have always sought solace during the winter months to escape the cold, recover, detox, go into hiding. I spent that entire wintry day lounging on and off rafts in their 90- to102-degree Olympic-size mineral pool, accompanied by a bottle of rosé. If ever a secret was worth sharing, this one surely is.

Indian Springs
1712 Lincoln Avenue
Calistoga, CA 94515
indianspringscalistoga.com

← TAKE A
MUD BATH

Tip!

GUESTS OF THE HOTEL OR SPA
CAN PARK BY THE HOT SPRINGS POOL
AND ORDER WINE POOLSIDE

→

THE GREAT HALL

**BE SURE
TO GET** ↘

Castello di Amorosa
4045 St. Helena Highway
Calistoga, CA 94515
castellodiamorosa.com

THE CROWD-PLEASER AWARD GOES TO: CASTELLO DI AMOROSA

Fairy tales are indeed alive and real in the Napa Valley. Once upon a time, a young medieval architecture enthusiast, Dario Sattui, owner of V. Sattui Winery in St. Helena, dreamed the impossible dream: to bring a piece of medieval Italy to the Napa Valley. The dream was Castello di Amorosa, which, in Italian, means Castle of Love, serving an array of exceptional Napa Valley wines. Overlooking Mount St. Helena in the quaint town of Calistoga, Castello di Amorosa is an otherworldly kingdom holding court on 170 acres. This 121,000-square-foot Tuscan castle is authentic to the bone—down to its one million handmade bricks recovered from fallen Hapsburg palaces, defensive towers, not one but two town squares, drawbridge and moat, chapel, and torture chamber (shhh!). What took Mr. Sattui fifteen years to build confidently grants guests entry to one of the most visited attractions in all the valley.

EATERY: ANDIE'S CAFE (at the Classic Car Wash)

Andie's is an itty-bitty drive-through café—another blink-and-you-might-miss-it sort of place, tucked behind the Classic Car Wash by the outlet stores—that is a serious guilty pleasure, loaded with fat and trans fats and thousands of calories.

I first learned about Andie's years ago through my mother, who has an uncanny knack and nose for discovering the very best hamburgers in a fifty-mile radius. She is persnickety about her burgers and wants nothing to do with gourmet varieties. She is highly particular about the bun-to-meat ratio, and likes her burgers well done/borderline fried and smothered in mayonnaise. She is also a secret connoisseur of hot dogs and loves hers grilled, crunchy to the bite, in an extra-enriched hot dog bun–and Andie's is spot-on.

The café itself looks like something William Eggleston would have immortalized while photographing Los Alamos some thirty years ago, evoking a time when Napa Valley was a much simpler place. The patrons are of every variety and flavor, whose common thread is a love of honest and shameless nostalgia. In a land of overfanciful and overwrought food, their menu is delicious, straightforward, and inexpensive, rocking other favorites like egg sandwiches with crispy bacon on a potato bun, fresh-cut fries, and old-school club sandwiches.

Andie's Cafe
1042 Freeway Drive
Napa, CA 94558
andiescafenapavalley.com

Vintage Home
1201 Main Street
St. Helena, CA 94574
napavalleyvintagehome.com

Vintage Home is my favorite store come December 1, when it is transformed into an Austrian wonderland, giving the fabled Christmas market of Vienna a run for its money. Laura Rombauer, the proprietress, has curated the most enchanting Old World holiday emporium, loaded to the gills with brilliant, thoughtful, elegant gifts and tree ornaments. What takes me over the top is her extraordinary inventory of wooden crafts—Christmas pyramids of sizes; nutcrackers; candelabras; and wooden incense smokers.

Every year my husband and I collect a new wooden heirloom. After anticipating this new purchase for months, on December 1, we arrive to inspect all the wooden loot, mercilessly analyzing which new prospect would fit in best with our house, family, or other wooden friends. And then we bring it home as if it were an original Picasso. From there, we assemble our entire collection on a table in the front foyer. Then we all congregate around the table to light the colored candles and marvel at the magic illuminating the room.

This spectacular extravaganza is what indelible memories, ceremonies, and rituals are all about.

THOMAS
KELLER

Introducing

THE FOODIE

THOMAS KELLER

with

JOEL GOTT

and

SAM GODFREY

THOMAS KELLER

Thomas Keller is an award-winning chef, restaurateur, and cookbook author. He is basically the Meryl Streep of the culinary universe and needs little introduction. The truth is, it is hard to do a book about the Napa Valley and not have Thomas direct the narrative because he *is* the narrative and is one of a handful of people who cast a worldwide spotlight on the valley. He has been a catalyst for the art of excellence and finesse in every realm he inhabits and has audaciously raised the bar for everyone in the valley: the winery proprietors, the farmers, the vendors, the florists, the cheese mongers, the hoteliers, the limo drivers, the gardeners, the designers, the service staff. Everyone in our world is inspired by the way he has talked the talk and walked the walk—all these years. He singlehandedly transformed the American culinary landscape.

THOMAS'S
Daily
UNIFORM

I find a daily uniform to be essential. I have so many decisions to make each day, and so many people relying on me to answer questions and be present, that I can't waste time worrying about whether what I am wearing is comfortable or appropriate. Over the years, I have selected the uniform that is best for my work: my chef jacket by Bragard, my custom Isaia black work pants and my Clogmaster black clogs, which have been fitted to my feet. On special occasions I wear my custom Isaia chef jacket.

I first came to the Napa Valley for The French Laundry. It was 1992, and my friend let me know a restaurant in Yountville was for sale. As soon as I stepped into the courtyard through a trellis hung with climbing roses, I felt as though I'd been heading here my whole life.

Since that day, I have maintained that the Napa Valley is a perfect place for a restaurant—it's the only place in the country where people come specifically to drink excellent wines and eat fine food. But there's more to its appeal. In many cities, like New York, restaurants re-create an experience of a faraway place. In the Napa Valley, we have the opportunity to capture on our menus the place—the vineyards, the farm fields, the abundance—right outside our doors. The fresh produce every month of the year, the great wines—these set the tone and guide our expectations for our work and our lives.

Thomas's
GOOD-TIMES CAR

**1974 BMW
320i**

I still have the first new car I ever purchased. A 1974 BMW 320i. It was right when they started making the 3 Series to replace the 2002. My brother got one first, and I loved the way it looked. I still do. It's been fully restored, and it's the perfect ride for an afternoon drive through the valley.

THOMAS'S
Favorite
SECRET PAIRING

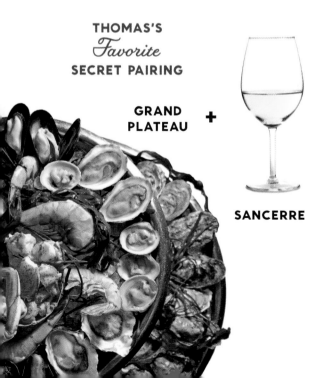

**GRAND
PLATEAU** **+**

SANCERRE

WHAT DID YOU WANT TO BE AS A CHILD?

A baseball player. I wanted to play shortstop for the New York Giants. As I grew older I wanted to be a chef. The earliest inspiration came from my mother, who was an avid home cook and a restaurant manager. The rituals and repetition resonated with me. My first job was as a dishwasher, and so much of what I learned in that role applies to being a cook: efficiency, organization, mastery through repetition. That's an important point to keep in mind. In the kitchen, you always want to try something new. But there really isn't anything new. What changes—what evolves and improves—is your own skill set, and that comes through repetition. I found true team spirit in the kitchen, and one that is as exhilarating to me as being on a baseball team.

Q&A WITH THOMAS KELLER

DESCRIBE YOUR DAILY MORNING ROUTINE.

I wake up without an alarm clock at seven A.M. This is easy to do when the sounds outside your window are of nature, as is the case in Napa Valley, instead of loud neighbors or traffic, as I would have in a city. I sometimes work out in the morning, if I know I won't be able to do so before dinner service at The French Laundry. For breakfast, I will have two hard-boiled eggs with one tablespoon of olive oil. I take my vitamins, make a double espresso, read the paper, and check in with my teams.

WHAT'S THE FIRST RECIPE YOU PERFECTED?

Hollandaise. I learned the technique over the course of a summer from my mentor, Roland Henin. But I wouldn't say "perfected" because there is no such thing as perfection. You can strive for perfection through repetition, by doing the same thing over and over, and you can find joy in the process. I truly think that if somebody prepares a dish they've never tried to make before and gets it right that first time, they're probably luckier than they are talented.

"Cooking is not about convenience, and it's not about shortcuts. Our hunger for the twenty-minute gourmet meal, for one-pot ease and prewashed, precut ingredients has severed our lifeline to the satisfactions of cooking. I don't have many favorite ingredients or tips because I'm not looking for convenience."

THOMAS'S FAVORITES

WHAT IS YOUR ONE FAVORITE ITEM ON THE FRENCH LAUNDRY, BOUCHON, AND AD HOC'S MENU?

I don't like to pick a favorite child. But I can recommend a few dishes that are the perfect choice for a particular occasion. If you're out with a bunch of friends, I would say meet up at Ad Hoc on a Monday fried chicken night. Everyone will pass plates around and share and have a great time. If you're out for a bit on your own, I would send you to Bouchon to sit at the bar and order the poulet rôti (roast chicken) with a glass of Sancerre. I don't dine at The French Laundry, but, of course, one dish that will always be special to me is the cornet. It's the first thing guests receive upon being seated. It looks like a miniature ice cream cone—we wanted its appearance to be unexpected—but the small cone is filled with salmon tartare and crème fraîche. It surprises and delights the eyes and the palate, and this is how I like to think of every guest starting their time at The French Laundry.

AD HOC'S
Fried Chicken

ICE CREAM

CUISINE

Japanese. I am fascinated by the precision and beauty of Japanese cuisine; the harmony is remarkable. French cuisine will always be the one that inspires and guides me the most. It is what my mentors cooked, it is what I look forward to traveling to eat, and it is what drives the menus of all of my restaurants on some level.

Coffee Toffee Bar Crunch from Ben & Jerry's! I am also a fan of more old-fashioned flavors like coffee and maple walnut.

BRAND OF COFFEE

Equator. Brooke McDonnell and Helen Russell's shared love for artisan coffee and their desire to have an impact on an industry with evolving social, economic, and environmental issues is profound. It's that commitment to building personal relationships with farmers and taking a hands-on approach that prompted us to collaborate with them. We serve our own unique blends of their coffee at all of our restaurants.

SHOP

Kelly's Filling Station. Yes, it's Yountville's only gas station, but just like so many businesses in Napa Valley, Kelly's has taken an essential need of travelers and infused it with hospitality and the best of what the area has to offer. Back Room Wines is a great wine shop in Napa and was started by a former sommelier at The French Laundry.

JUNK FOOD →

An In-N-Out burger with extra-crispy fries, but I don't consider this to be junk food!

THOMAS'S FAVORITES

VARIETAL OF TOMATO

We have forty varieties of tomatoes at The French Laundry Culinary Garden. Some of my favorites include heirlooms like the Kellogg's Breakfast or the Amish Red. The Sun Gold is a perennial favorite for everyone, and all the restaurants enjoy working with the Green Zebra.

FORTY VARIETIES AT THE FRENCH LAUNDRY CULINARY GARDEN

Fridge MVP

Dijon mustard. I prefer Edmond Fallot. I always have it on hand for making a vinaigrette, which is one of the simple things I think everyone should make, not buy. Oil, vinegar, mustard, lemon.

BEVERAGE GLASS →

At home, I use many of the same glasses we use at the restaurants, as they have withstood my tests for design and function. At The French Laundry, we use Riedel, Zalto, and Baccarat. We use Spiegelau at Ad Hoc for both stemless and flutes.

OFF-DUTY DRINK

**HITACHINO NEST
WHITE ALE**

**MACALLAN 25
(neat with a drop
or two of water)**

**CASA DRAGONES
BLANCO**

COOKBOOK →

I cite this book as the cookbook that most influenced me as a young cook. First published in the United States in 1974 but long out of print, Fernand Point's page-turner cookbook was republished in 2008, and I was honored to offer a foreword for that edition. The book is half recipes, half stories, and the stories about Point himself are remarkable and beautifully told. It's as inspirational to read as it is to cook from.

Food CRAVE

"Roast chicken, it is as wholesome as it is delicious.
It's a recipe I like to encourage people to try for a number
of different reasons. It's something that crosses economic,
social, and geographic boundaries. Roast chicken is so
satisfying: the aromas as it's roasting, and then, of course,
the different textures and flavors as you eat it. I think being
able to roast a chicken really well is something that will
serve someone for a long, long time."

My Favorite Simple Roast Chicken (Mon Poulet Rôti)
Serves 2 to 4

One 2- to 3-pound farm-raised chicken
Kosher salt and freshly ground black pepper
2 teaspoons minced thyme (optional)
Unsalted butter
Dijon mustard
Preheat the oven to 450°F. Rinse the chicken, then dry it very well with paper
towels, inside and out. The less it steams, the drier the heat, the better.

Salt and pepper the cavity, then truss the bird. Trussing is not difficult,
and if you roast chicken often, it's a good technique to feel comfortable
with. When you truss a bird, the wings and legs stay close to the body; the
ends of the drumsticks cover the top of the breast and keep it from drying
out. Trussing helps the chicken to cook evenly, and it also makes for a more
beautiful roasted bird.

Now, salt the chicken-I like to rain the salt over the bird so that it has a
nice uniform coating that will result in a crisp, salty, flavorful skin (about
1 tablespoon). When it's cooked, you should still be able to make out the salt
baked onto the crisp skin. Season to taste with pepper.

Place the chicken in a sauté pan or roasting pan and, when the oven is up to
temperature, put the chicken in the oven. I leave it alone-I don't baste it,
I don't add butter; you can if you wish, but I feel this creates steam, which
I don't want. Roast it until it's done, 50 to 60 minutes. Remove it from the
oven and add the thyme, if using, to the pan. Baste the chicken with the juices
and thyme and let it rest for 15 minutes on a cutting board.

Remove the twine. Separate the middle wing joint and eat that immediately.
Remove the legs and thighs. I like to take off the backbone and eat one of the
oysters, the two succulent morsels of meat embedded here, and give the other
to the person I'm cooking with. But I take the chicken butt for myself. I could
never understand why my brothers always fought over that triangular tip-until
one day I got the crispy, juicy fat myself. These are the cook's rewards. Cut
the breast down the middle and serve it on the bone, with one wing joint still
attached to each. The preparation is not meant to be superelegant. Slather the
meat with fresh butter. Serve with mustard on the side and, if you wish, a
simple green salad. You'll start using a knife and fork, but finish with your
fingers, because it's so good.

THOMAS'S FAVORITES

Signature GIFT

I like to give someone a book that speaks to who they are. Or speaks to their interests or their personality. When a person on our staff celebrates a milestone, I like to give that person a book. For a young chef, it might be Fernand Point's *Ma Gastronomie* or Michael Ruhlman's *The Soul of a Chef*. For someone on my management team, it might be Coach John Wooden's *Wooden: A Lifetime of Observations and Reflections On and Off the Court*—his wisdom is timeless and we often reference his quotes in our kitchens.

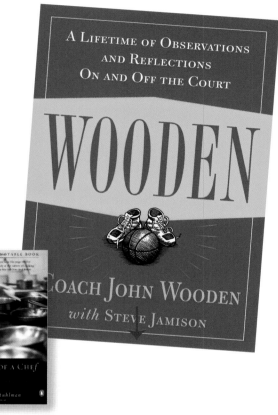

The → PICNIC

A good baguette is the most important thing. Some saucisson, cornichons, pâté grand-père, French radishes with butter (Président), fleur de sel, and an Opinel knife. A chilled rosé from Provence or a Beaujolais is also essential, and don't forget a wine opener, Govino plastic wineglasses, a serviette, and a cozy blanket.

For dessert, I pack cherries or green grapes or the fruit of the season. Playing cards or a backgammon set are nice touches. And just like in the kitchen, no music. Enjoy the sound of nature and your companion.

CORNICHONS

ENTERTAINMENT

SAUCISSON

KNIFE

BUTTER

CORKSCREW

Must-Have
PICNIC ITEMS

**FRENCH
RADISHES**

GOVINO

ROSÉ

FLEUR DE SEL

A GOOD BAGUETTE

BLANKET

Introducing
JOEL GOTT
THE SERIAL ENTREPRENEUR

Ok, Joel is the local consigliere—the one to call in a jam, and also the one to bounce off good ideas and bad ones, too. Professionally, Joel is a wunderkind entrepreneur with booming restaurant and wine businesses—a kind of magical combination that is as rare as hen's teeth. Ideas are his thing. Gott's Roadside—née Taylor's Refresher—reinvented the roadside burger stand; made it straight-up cool by incorporating California perspective, high-quality ingredients, and modern yet retro design. In the wine world, Joel Gott wines are one of the great success stories in the valley. After two decades, Gott's Roadside still remains a must-visit destination in the valley by those in the know, those not in the know, and those looking to be charmed.

JOEL GOTT

HOW DID YOU END UP IN NAPA?

I was born in Napa Valley, but before moving here as an adult I was living in Tahoe as a ski bum. My dad convinced my brother and me to borrow money from him to buy Palisades Market in Calistoga to get us living closer to them. I haven't been able to leave since.

WOULD YOU CALL YOURSELF A VINTNER? RESTAURATEUR? ENTREPRENEUR? OR WHAT?

"AN *entrepreneur,*
a **WINE & FOOD** *guy,*
a **GUY WITH** *crazy* **IDEAS . . ."**

HOW AND WHEN DID TAYLOR'S/GOTT'S START?

In 1999, my brother and I were running Palisades Market in Calistoga when we heard Taylor's Refresher in St. Helena was up for lease. We saw it as a potential outpost/produce stand and ended up taking it all on (car wash included) and serving our favorite California foods. Keep in mind, we were in our twenties, so this meant that the burgers and sandwiches we'd eaten while living in Carmel, Santa Barbara, and Los Angeles were our inspiration.

Q&A with Joel

WHY DO YOU THINK GOTT'S RESONATES SO INTENSELY?
WHAT WOULD YOU SAY IS THE SECRET SAUCE OF ITS SUCCESS?
It's familiar. It's comfortable. And yet it's fresh and evolves. The "secret sauce" is trying really hard. Every year the food (and everything else) gets better.

WHO ARE YOUR CUSTOMERS?
Families, office workers, tourists ... everyone.

HOW MANY GOTT'S ROADSIDES ARE THERE TODAY?
Four. St. Helena, San Francisco's Ferry Building, Napa's Oxbow Public Market, and Town & Country Village in Palo Alto.

WHAT IS THE MOST POPULAR MENU ITEM?
The cheeseburger. Nothing else comes close.

TELL ME WHY YOUR BEER AND WINE LINEUP IS SO AWESOME
We really like beer and wine, so it matters. We taste through a crazy number of wines to find the best ones for a burger price point. Beers are a little easier, but really the great part about the program is that it's a heavily edited list, which makes it hard to go wrong.

ARCHITECTURE AND GRAPHIC DESIGN HAVE ALWAYS BEEN CORNERSTONES OF YOUR CONCEPT. HOW DID THEY COME TOGETHER? HOW DID IT EVOLVE?

We started with clip art and a rebuilt burger stand. Over the years I've worked with architects and designers and along the way became more knowledgeable and formed my own opinions. With Gott's, I think we realized how special and iconic the white burger stand was. We do our best to stay true to that classic aesthetic while keeping it relevant and fresh-feeling at the same time.

HOW TO MAKE A WORLD-CLASS BURGER
by JOEL GOTT

THE BEEF
We use Niman Ranch at the restaurants, but just start with good-quality ground beef with an 80:20 meat-to-fat ratio and a medium grind, and don't overwork the patties.

SEASONING
Keep it simple.
Salt and pepper.

CHEESE
American

CONDIMENTS
Flavored mayonnaise
is usually the best.

SPECIAL SAUCE
Mayonnaise, ketchup,
mustard, relish, and spices

BUN
Nothing too delicate (like brioche) or too tough. We use an egg bun from Panorama Bakery, but potato buns are also great for burgers. Alexis Baking Company (ABC) in Napa makes exceptional ones.

HOW TO MAKE A WORLD-CLASS SHAKE
by JOEL GOTT

ICE CREAM
Three Twins. You want great, clean flavors that aren't overly sweet.

TOPPINGS
Pure or with chocolate sauce

MILK
By weight you should shoot for a 3:1 ice-cream-to-milk ratio. And use whole milk.

"The biggest secret is how much ice cream goes into each shake. You don't want to know."

JOEL'S FAVORITES

RESTAURANT TO EAT OUT AT FOR YOUR BIRTHDAY?

The roast chicken at Press is exceptional. Mustards Grill has an amazing curried calamari salad, a great tostada, and one of the best lemon meringue pies. I'd never pass up a meal at The French Laundry or Chez Panisse. I love food. It's hard to pick just one place.

← **MUSTARDS'S** *famous* **LEMON-LIME TART**

WATERING HOLE?

I meet friends for a drink at local restaurants like Terra, Cook, and Cindy's.

JOEL GOTT

MARKET/WINE SHOP/GROCERY STORE

Oxbow Public Market for produce and meat, Sunshine for groceries and Kermit Lynch for wine

IF YOU COULD GET ONE RESERVATION ON A MOMENT'S NOTICE IN NAPA, WHERE WOULD IT BE?

The French Laundry

All about
SAM GODFREY
BAKER TO THE STARS

 Sam Godfrey is the proprietor of Perfect Endings in Napa Valley and is also known around the world as Oprah's favorite baker. Sam is revered for his magnificent creations and confections, which inspired an entire universe of bakers to deliver cakes that looked every bit as good as they taste. In the world of fantasy cakes, that is a tall order. For my wedding, Sam created a sublime cake buffet that looked straight out of an old-fashioned bake sale and featured ten different types of vintage cakes, all using his grandmother's coveted recipes. They looked like cakes made by your grandmother, with love. For the bride and groom, he made a heart-shaped red velvet cake, decorated with our initials in Red Hots! It was perfection.

SAM GODFREY

HOW DOES IT FEEL TO BE KNOWN AS OPRAH'S BAKER?

Well, Miss Oprah has been quite effusive in describing my work and me for the past sixteen years. I still cannot believe she even knows who I am. Compliments make me uncomfortable, and I do not like being the center of attention, so adjusting to the magnitude of her support has been a journey, but a glorious journey indeed. She has taken my cakes and pies around the world—literally—and made them the centerpiece of her celebrations. I am humbled by her generosity, and grateful for the gift of Oprah Winfrey.

WHO TAUGHT YOU TO BAKE?

Her name was Pearl, and she was born and raised in Little Rock, Arkansas. I was her first grandchild and favorite guinea pig. She was a phenomenal cook and extraordinary baker who was overjoyed when I received a scholarship to Cordon Bleu, Paris, because it meant that I would learn to bake the "proper way." I left Paris after eleven days when I learned she was terminally ill and never went back or sought any formal training. One of my goals is to go to culinary school to be properly trained, but I must admit that it is deliciously ironic that baking "mama's way" has pleased so many people. I'm just the liaison . . . the talent was hers.

GROWING UP, WAS BAKING YOUR SPECIALTY?

I baked the full repertoire of Southern delicacies—especially sweet potato and buttermilk pies, peach cobbler, and coconut cake—until I wandered into Alice Medrich's groundbreaking Cocolat dessert shop in Berkeley at age eleven. That was my Willy Wonka moment . . . I had never seen European pastry before. The refinement, the restraint and sophistication. I inhaled it! This was the start of what Mama most affectionately called my "___ damn mousse" phase!

At age twelve I marched into the Baptist church potluck—the temple of red velvet cake and pecan pie—with a huge (green Tupperware!) bowl of chocolate mousse . . . that I didn't receive the Medal of Honor for such bravery remains *the* greatest slight of the twentieth century!

HOW DID YOU DECIDE TO SET UP YOUR BUSINESS IN NAPA, OF ALL PLACES? WHEN? WHY WAS IT IMPORTANT? WHY NOT SAN FRANCISCO?

Around 1990, I was recruited to Napa as a tennis pro and taught tennis there for several years before opening my business. I'd often bake things for my students, some of whom were from renowned wine families. They started to request desserts for family and special events, and word spread. The response to my baking was encouraging by those who first became acquainted with me as a tennis pro, which led me to set up shop in Napa; but encounters I had with buyers and event professionals were nightmares. Truthfully, I stayed in Napa Valley out of defiance.

WHAT ARE YOU KNOWN FOR TODAY?

I think we will always be known first and foremost as bakers of cake—of all kinds.

HOW ARE WEDDING CAKE TRENDS DIFFERENT NOW, COMPARED WITH TEN YEARS AGO?

I have always hoped that pastry chefs would finally understand that the inside of the cake is every bit as important as the exterior . . . that it is, in fact, dessert and it should taste extraordinary. Unfortunately, with the advent of the "celebrity" chef and Food Network competitions, taste is a distant second to artistry. I will make a cake that looks like the Taj Mahal . . . I've learned that they have their place. It should not, however, taste like the Taj Mahal!

WHAT IS YOUR MOST POPULAR CAKE?

It's probably a tie between our Chocolate Candy Bar cake and our Plain Jane, which is my homage to Safeway's white layer cake with vanilla frosting. We make so many light and luscious things, refined and with a European tilt, but Americana gets 'em every time!

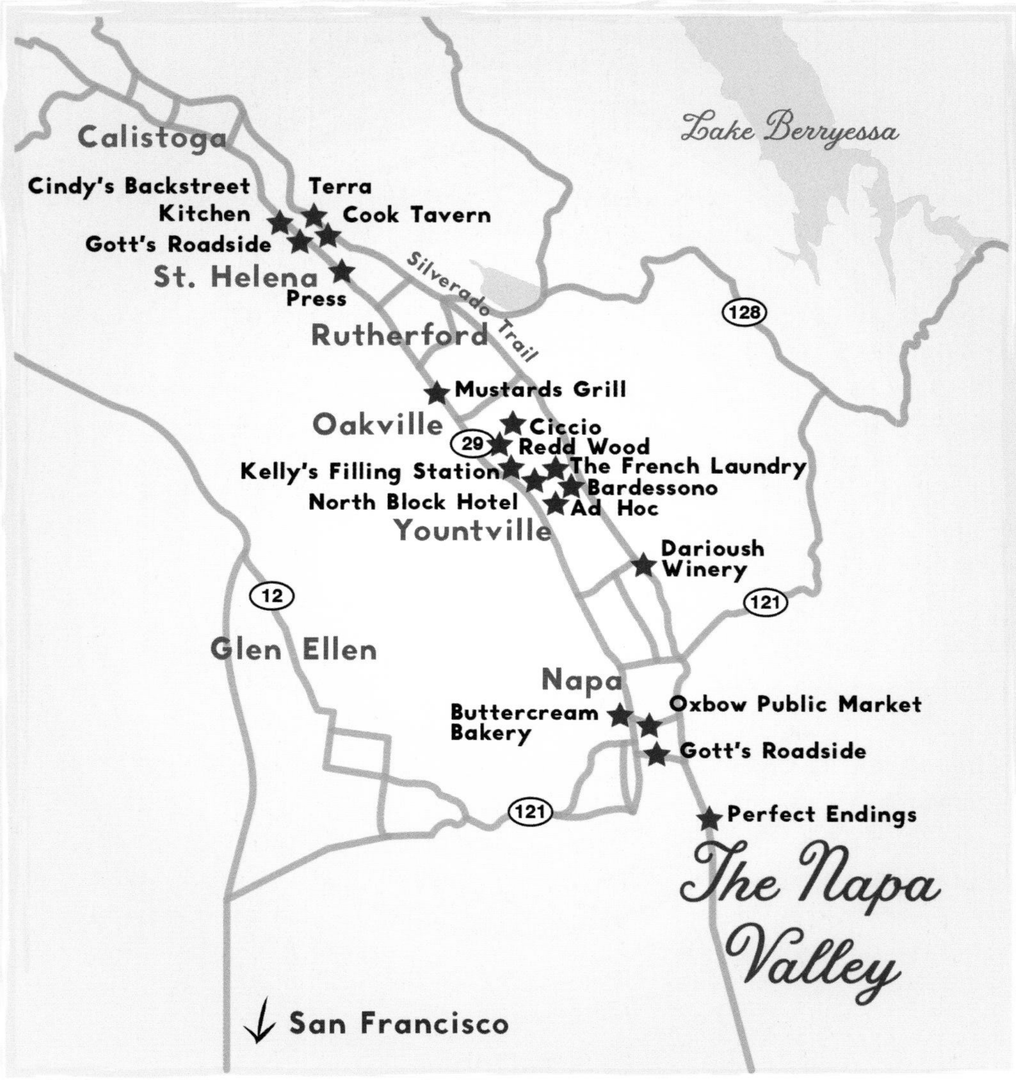

Calistoga

Cindy's Backstreet
Kitchen ★ ★ Terra
★ ★ Cook Tavern
Gott's Roadside ★ ★
St. Helena ★
Press

Silverado Trail

Rutherford

128

★ Mustards Grill

Oakville
★ Ciccio
29 ★ Redd Wood
Kelly's Filling Station ★ ★ ★ The French Laundry
★ ★ Bardessono
North Block Hotel ★ ★ Ad Hoc
Yountville

★ Darioush
Winery

121

12

Glen Ellen

Napa
Buttercream ★ ★ Oxbow Public Market
Bakery
★ Gott's Roadside

121
★ Perfect Endings

*The Napa
Valley*

↓ San Francisco

Lake Berryessa

Alexis's
FOODIE
GUIDE

WHERE TO STAY

WHERE TO EAT

WHERE TO WINE

and

MUSTN'T MISS

LODGING: BARDESSONO

Bardessono
6526 Yount Street
Yountville, CA 94599
bardessono.com

There is nothing I like more than landing somewhere and immediately becoming a part of a neighborhood and beat. In the thick of Yountville, Bardessono Hotel & Spa is just that kind of place. Bardessono, the only Platinum LEED–certified hotel in California, is thoughtfully adorned with the latest twenty-first-century gadgetry (my personal favorite are the super-fancy Toto toilets in the restroom by the bar). If that doesn't grab you, the hotel graciously accepts pets, offers in-room spa services, a real bar and restaurant called Lucy, a rooftop pool, and at-the-ready cruiser bikes. Within a few minutes' walk from your front door is The French Laundry, Bouchon Bakery, Bistro Jeanty, Redd, Bottega, Ad Hoc, Redd Wood, and Ciccio.

THE WINERY: DARIOUSH

Darioush Winery is the dream of Darioush Khaledi and an homage to wine's historic beginnings in the Fertile Crescent, which comprises some of modern-day Iran, where Darioush was born. The first thing to notice upon driving up to the winery is the striking Persian columns that impose from the entrance, which is supposed to evoke the ancient city of Persepolis, and, inside, Persian rugs and rich, colorful textiles that evoke the spirit and culture of the Middle East. Though Darioush's wines are made from traditional varietals that thrive in Napa Valley—including Cabernet, Cab Franc, Shiraz, and Viognier, instead of indigenous varietals from near the Caucasus region, they are very distinct in nature and every bit as exciting as the nontraditional architecture of the winery. A must.

Darioush Vineyards
4240 Silverado Trail
Napa, CA 94558
darioush.com

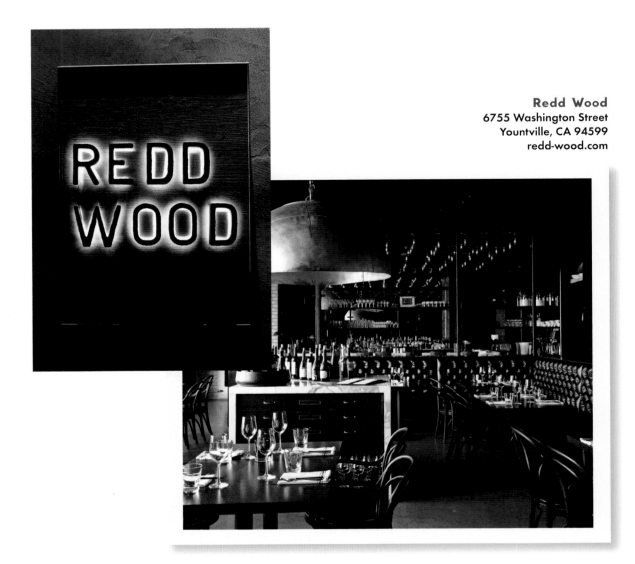

Redd Wood
6755 Washington Street
Yountville, CA 94599
redd-wood.com

SOME OF THOMAS KELLER'S FAVORITE RESTAURANTS

Richard is a good friend and talented chef who has a real understanding of Italian cuisine. I am a big fan of his pizzas; you can't go wrong with the classic tomato (without cheese) or the margherita pizza, a house-made pasta dish, and the chopped salad. Ciccio in Yountville is another favorite. Their menu changes every few days, but you can always count on a Negroni and any of their wood-fired appetizers, such as the artichokes. The Altamuras are a wonderful family and are very hospitable to guests and neighbors. For steak, I recommend Press in St. Helena. Their selection of California Reserve USDA Prime from Bryan Flannery is outstanding. Their wine list is also spectacular.

Ciccio
6770 Washington Street
Yountville, CA 94599
ciccionapavalley.com

Press
587 St. Helena Highway
St. Helena, CA 94574
pressnapavalley.com

MUSTN'T MISS: TFL GARDEN

I arrived at dusk to meet the head gardener of The French Laundry garden with a huge entourage in tow: my two children, cousin, husband, babysitter, and photographer. I usually can bribe only one of them to join me on such explorations, but they were *all* desperate to discover every inch of Thomas Keller's enchanting and inspiring garden, cornstalks, berry patches, chicken coop, and greenhouse. Like most residents of the valley, we have watched with curiosity and delight as Thomas's crew of five full-time gardeners lovingly tamed and transformed a two-acre parcel of raw land into a flourishing urban garden in the middle of Yountville, right in front of The French Laundry.

As with all things Thomas Keller, there is a brilliant and bewitching method to his madness thriving in his fifty-three meticulous vegetable patches, which service not only TFL, but Bouchon and Ad Hoc as well. There were at least twenty-five tomato varieties, hominy grown from stashed Peruvian seeds, Cinderella pumpkins, Jerusalem artichokes, Padrón peppers, baby zucchini, broccoli, kale, and a half dozen types of cucumbers and fingerlings. All varieties are planted and grown in a checkerboard grid, on constant rotation, for best gardening and soil practices.

As we walked around, we tasted the craziest things: oyster leaves, which taste just like an oyster; stevia leaves, which are so absurdly sweet that the taste refuses to leave your palate; ground cherries; and albino strawberries. Yet all paths in the garden led my group to the henhouse (a mini replica of the actual French Laundry) and dozens of the most perfectly coiffed Bantam-Cochins.

ANDY + KATE SPADE

Introducing

THE SUMMER FOLK

KATE & ANDY SPADE

with

CLAIBORNE SWANSON FRANK

Everyone knows the urban legend of Kate Spade: Kate Brosnahan and Andy Spade first met while working at Johnson and Company, a men's clothing store, while at Arizona State. After graduating, they combined their names and started their eponymous handbag line out of a tiny studio apartment they shared—and created a magical empire celebrating life as they saw it!

The Spades have spent their adult lives living as true New Yorkers, inspiring and inhabiting the fashion world through their iconic companies, Kate Spade and Jack Spade, and their latest adventure, Frances Valentine. Together, like partners in crime, they charmed a whole generation to live with exuberance, humor, and style. Kate and Andy have been summer residents in the Napa Valley for the last decade, setting up shop there during the months of July and August.

KATE: I adore living in New York City, but Napa is our ultimate escape. People are so fascinated that we would go so far instead of going to Long Island, which is a few hours' drive away. Well . . . that's the point! We have lazy days spent by the pool, watching our daughter play tennis and having very casual and intimate lunches and dinners with our friends. It is truly the opposite of New York—and the Hamptons, for that matter. A refreshing atmosphere in the most beautiful setting!

As a family we *love* to play badminton and Ping-Pong—all the gloves come off! Ha! We also love to ride our bikes, which is quite a luxury for us New Yorkers. Even something as simple as just driving around listening to the radio is something we like to do because we don't do it in New York. There, the taxi driver determines what you listen to, so in Napa, we play the music loudly and sing along poorly! And don't get me started on the food and wine! There's nowhere to start or end on that subject!

ANDY'S
Favorite
SECRET
PAIRING

+

**PARLIAMENT
ULTRA LIGHTS**

**JACK QUINN
WINE**

**VINTAGE
INDIAN
MOTORCYCLE**

Andy's
GOOD-TIMES WHEELS

"I have always wanted to do
a photo book of my many
Napa Instagram photos and call it:

Running, Smoking, Swimming

and Drinking, and

Sometimes a Little Bit of Tennis."

–Andy Spade

Q&A WITH ANDY SPADE

WHAT DID YOU WANT TO BE AS A CHILD?
I had two career aspirations as a child: to be a fifth-grade teacher and/or a professional skateboarder.

BIRTH SIGNS?
I am a Taurus and Kate is a Capricorn. People tell me that's a good thing.

FAVORITE SEASON IN THE VALLEY AND WHY?
Summer, but we also love the fall, especially September and October during harvest when the mustard seed is in full bloom

St. Helena Skate Park

FAVORITE WATERING HOLE?

PANCHA'S IN YOUNTVILLE

FAVORITE AFTERNOON

Meadowood by the kiddie pool, drinking Southsides and eating cheeseburgers while plunked down on the lawn and "magazining." Selections could include everything from *World of Interiors* to *Fast Company*.

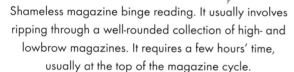

"MAGAZINING"

Shameless magazine binge reading. It usually involves ripping through a well-rounded collection of high- and lowbrow magazines. It requires a few hours' time, usually at the top of the magazine cycle.

ANDY'S
Go-To Gift

**MODERN HOUSE WINES—
I ESPECIALLY LIKE
PLEASE FORGIVE ME**

**NAPA VALLEY
OLIVE OIL**

Kelly's Filling Station
6795 Washington Street
Yountville, CA 94599

ANDY'S →
Go-To Treat

I go there for excellent coffee, cool Kelly's souvenir T-shirts, super-decent wine selection, and the best magazine and newspaper selection, including *Kinfolk* and *Diner Journal*, two great, hard-to-find magazines. And it's the only place you can get Fuller's Cheesy Puffs in jalapeño flavor.

Kate's SUMMER FOLK NECESSITIES

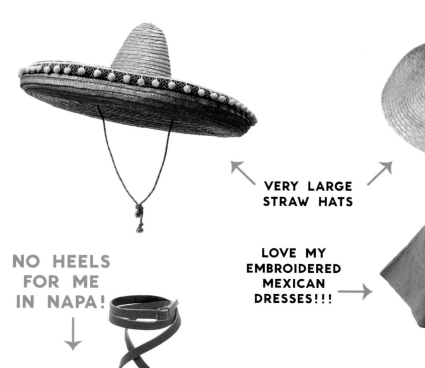

VERY LARGE STRAW HATS

LOVE MY EMBROIDERED MEXICAN DRESSES!!!

NO HEELS FOR ME IN NAPA!

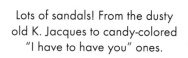

Lots of sandals! From the dusty old K. Jacques to candy-colored "I have to have you" ones.

SHORT AND LONG IN LOTS OF COLORS!

ACCESSORIES

I favor a mishmash of interesting jewelry that I can wear poolside or to dinner. It must be versatile. This is the jewelry I wore all summer and have not taken off. I buy a lot of ethnic jewelry and happen to be in a bit of a gypsy jewelry look. I go from loving lots of beaded necklaces, then to rings and bracelets or an interesting pair of earrings to nothing at all. I'm not crazy about diamonds unless they're modestly mixed with other materials like turquoise, gold, or coral.

**FRANCES VALENTINE
SQUARE STRAW TOTE**

THE *Southside*

vodka
fresh-squeezed lemons
simple syrup
muddled mint
sparkling water

**THE PERFECT
SUMMER COCKTAIL**

PAJAMAS

I am not just saying this because Andy owns the company, but I bring a ton of Sleepy Jones pajamas, and honestly, I can go an entire day wearing them at home, by the pool, playing Ping-Pong, eating dinner, and then watching a good movie.

FULL SKIRTS

Can be daywear or dressed up with jewelry and a cashmere sweater at night

**CHOCOLATE
BOUCHONS**

← WHO CAN
RESIST?

KATE'S GO-TO DINNER PARTY

Kate's
GO-TO DECOR

Must have
STRONG COLOR!

There is nothing I love more than strong color. Pink paper plates, orange paper napkins, pink and orange poppies, striped straws with Christmas lights around the table makes any night of the week special.

Favorite →
BEVERAGE GLASS

I love Reidel Os. They are all-purpose and perfect for wine, cocktails, sodas, lemonade, water. Everyone is happy.

Favorite
HORS D'OEUVRE

ONION DIP
Made with sour cream and the powder stuff,
all stirred together, served with Ruffles potato chips

Favorite
← **DESSERTS** →

Homemade cakes and
brownies from the box,
Twizzlers, and Kit Kats

PARTY TRICK

← **WE MAKE**
Mix Tapes →

Mostly blues and jazz during dinner, and the programming gets progressively looser as the night goes on

CLAIBORNE SWANSON FRANK
THE PHOTOGRAPHER

My sister Claiborne is a photographer whose books include *American Beauty* and *Young Hollywood*. What sets her work apart is her commitment to capturing a woman's very best self . . . Not her six A.M. self in a robe; not her Tuesday-night self over a stove; not her weekend self, driving a minivan. Claiborne is possessed by capturing the minute details that tell her subject's life story—favorite or meaningful choice of dress, jewelry, and accessories while sitting in the environs that magnify the story being shared. The end portrait is an exercise in celebrating the sum of the parts that make us all truly individual.

I have always joked that these portraits are the kinds of photos you want to have at your bedside in the nursing home at eighty-five—proof of the life you so proudly lived, and proof you looked damn good while living it.

My sister Claiborne and her husband James

YOU ARE EXPERT AT...

Portraiture. For me, it is a window into one's soul and a means through which we can express who we are. The portrait has the power tell a story, to inspire, to document a life. The portrait allows us to proclaim, "I was here and this is who I was." When this life is over, I feel deeply that the portrait is the most powerful artifact we will have of our lives and the person we were and wanted to be.

HOW DID YOU HONE IN ON THIS NICHE?

As a young child, I was always mesmerized by images of women in magazines. I remember often wondering who they were and how they lived their lives. I ripped endless photos out of the pages and covered the walls of my bedroom with them. I loved photography. I loved pictures. I loved beauty. Throughout my adolescence, I remember devouring *Vogue* and not really reading the articles but just studying the pictures. Pictures have moved me deeply for as long as I can remember, and inspired me to dream. I think the portrait was the extension of this dream of self and the ability, through a portrait, to tell a story of a life.

WHEN DID YOU FIRST PICK UP A CAMERA? WHAT WERE YOU PHOTOGRAPHING THEN?

My mom (also a photographer) would always give me her camera when we visited Europe during my high school years, but I really fell in love with the practice when I started taking portraits of my best friends and sisters in my early twenties. I was doing the same thing then that I do now: dressing up my friends and taking pictures.

INSTAGRAMMING
WITH
CLAIBORNE...

Favorite
FILTER?
Valencia and Sierra

Favorite
TIME OF DAY?
Sunrise and sunset

WHAT MAKES NAPA AN INSTAGRAMMER'S WONDERLAND?
The way the light hits the land, the awesome beauty of the valley, and the moments in between.

WHICH PARTS OF THE VALLEY DO YOU WANDER TO?
I grew up on the valley floor so I am used to the feeling of being surrounded by mountains. I love the peace and the open space of the valley floor—and the diversity of landscape in Napa. One minute you could be in the vineyards on a dirt road and the next minute you could be on a trail overlooking a lake.

WHAT STORY ARE YOU TRYING TO CAPTURE?
The story of my life and the people and the places I love. Photography is a way I hold on to these moments. When this ride is over, these images and stories will live on, and I like the feeling of knowing that.

CLAIBORNE SWANSON FRANK

FAVORITE SEASON?

We grew up spending our summers in Napa. It was my most favorite time of year. Summer was when we lived deeply and fully. Those months in Napa marked a time when I could lose myself and focus on being . . . being alive and free without a care in the world.

WHAT ARE THE DOMINANT THEMES AND SUBJECTS IN YOUR WORK?

My subjects are nature, children, family, dogs, open fields, barns, and old cars, and the themes I'm interested in are family, beauty, and how people live.

TOP FIVE INSTAGRAM DESTINATIONS

Dirt roads

Vineyards

Lake Hennessey

My parents' property

White Sulphur Springs

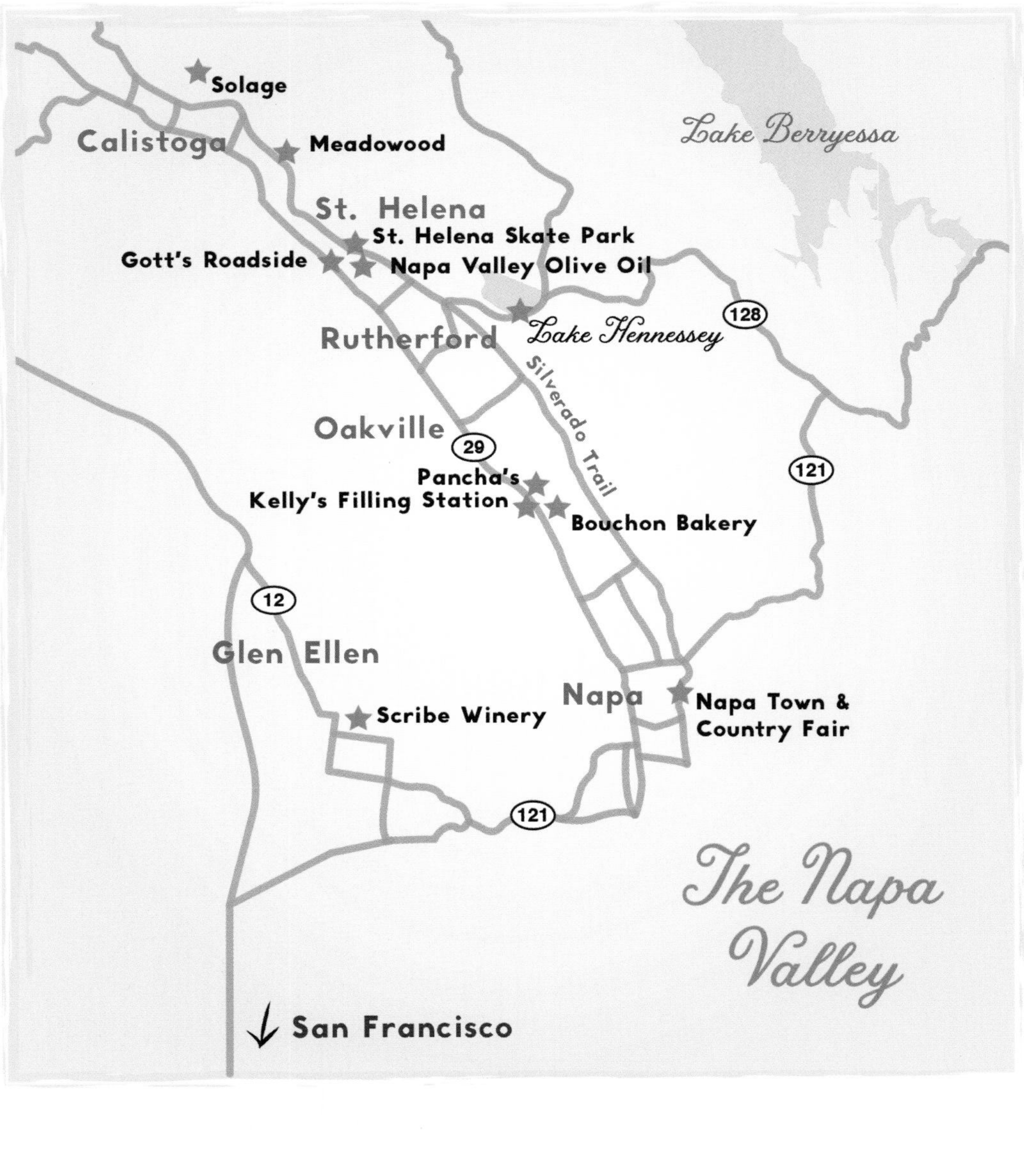

Solage

Calistoga

Meadowood

Lake Berryessa

St. Helena

St. Helena Skate Park

Napa Valley Olive Oil

Gott's Roadside

Rutherford   *Lake Hennessey*

128

Silverado Trail

Oakville

29

Pancha's

Kelly's Filling Station

Bouchon Bakery

121

12

Glen Ellen

Napa

Scribe Winery

Napa Town &
Country Fair

121

↓ San Francisco

*The Napa
Valley*

Alexis's

SUMMER FOLK
GUIDE

WHERE TO STAY
WHERE TO EAT
WHERE TO WINE

and

MUSTN'T MISS

LODGING: SOLAGE

Solage Resort in Calistoga is the little sister property to the ultra-luxurious Calistoga Ranch and Auberge du Soleil, only Solage has a hipper, more vibrant feel than its siblings. With eighty-nine cottage rooms designed by architect Howard Backen, Solage understands good vacationing and the importance of good vibes. From the Olympic-size lap pool to the manicured bocce ball court to the alfesco dining and cocktail patios under a canopy of trees, outdoors at the Solage is where it's at. And once you've sufficiently worn yourself out, make your way back to Solbar's inventive farm-to-table restaurant. It'd be the perfect ending to a lovely day.

Calistoga is home to some of the best mineral springs in the world, so it's no surprise that Solage's twenty-thousand-square-foot spa's specialty is mud baths, harnessing the power of the nearby geothermal springs to purify and rejuvenate your body. After all, isn't that what a vacation in wine country is all about?

Solage
55 Silverado Trail North
Calistoga, CA 94515
solage.aubergeresorts.com

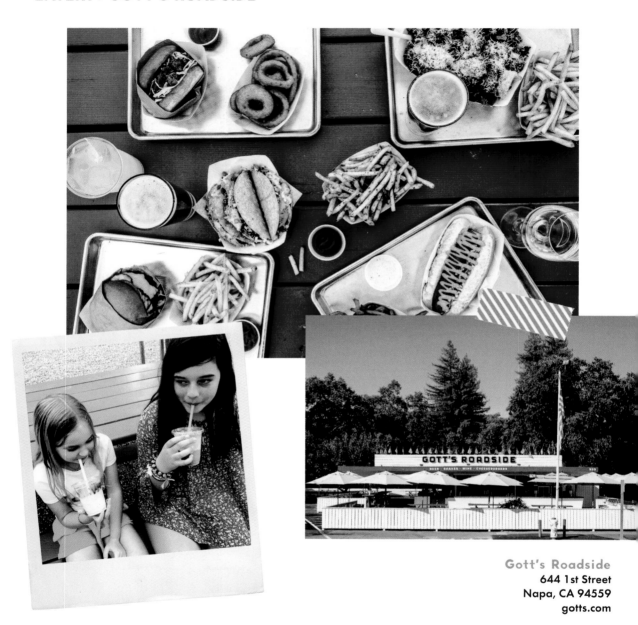

Gott's Roadside
644 1st Street
Napa, CA 94559
gotts.com

Gott's Roadside instantly says "Napa" to me and is a modern-day slice of Americana that makes every day of summer feel like the Fourth of July! For us, an early lunch at Gott's, at least once a weekend, is serious business. I covet the regular burger with extra-special sauce, the sweet potato fries, and the espresso bean shake, made with Three Twins ice cream. A visit to Gott's is all about timing: either go for an early or late lunch. But do yourself a favor; do not show up between noon and 1:30 P.M. because it's so crowded.

Scribe Winery
2100 Denmark Street
Sonoma, CA 95476
scribewinery.com

Like most, I am always eager for word-of-mouth recommendations from friends in the know. Following that thread, I kept seeing post after Instagram post of GOOD TIMES spent at Scribe—from legions of people I follow and I respect. Photos capturing dirt roads, party tents, Ford trucks, tree lanterns and swings, vintage picnic tables, and eclectic winemaker dinner parties in Napa, San Francisco, Brooklyn, Los Angeles. Unfiltered, unvarnished, straight-up old-school photos that presented a modern grassroots approach to wine and agrarian life in the twenty-first century.

Scribe, while not directly in Napa, is one of the emerging stars of Sonoma Valley. Run by two young brothers, Andrew and Adam Mariani, Scribe is . . . different. While the brothers are known for making beautiful Chardonnays, Pinot Noirs, and Cabernets, they are definitely not risk-averse, as they create exceptional small productions of lesser-known varietals such as Sylvaner, a grape native to Germany, and St. Laurent, a varietal with Austrian heritage—all the reasons bohemians, foodies, tastemakers, oenophiles, and summer folk come to wine country!

MUSTN'T MISS: NAPA TOWN & COUNTRY FAIR

Napa Valley has two classic fairs in the summer—the Napa County Fair over the Fourth of July in Calistoga, and the Napa Town & Country Fair in mid-August. The Town & Country Fair is an old-fashioned operation under the most gorgeous alley of trees in downtown Napa with clown acts, a major 4-H production, a petting zoo, snowball stands, tons of rides, kitschy vendors, and every manner of fried goodness.

MY KIDS & I
especially love

The guy who makes the airbrushed T-shirts,
the chocolate-covered bacon booth,
mini doughnuts by the bucket,
corn dogs,
and the super slide

Napa Town &
Country Fair
575 3rd Street
Napa, CA 94559
napavalleyexpo.com

CARLO
MONDAVI

Introducing

THE OENOPHILE
CARLO MONDAVI
with
AGUSTIN FRANCISCO HUNEEUS JR.

CARLO MONDAVI

Grandson of Robert Mondavi, Carlo Mondavi is the heir to the Mondavi legacy—the most defining influence in the American wine industry to date. Every early Napa Valley story, footnote, or urban legend points back to Robert, Michael, and Tim Mondavi—a family of sheer multigenerational talent and vision that brought worldwide recognition of Napa Valley. Like his grandfather and father, Carlo Mondavi is equal parts entrepreneur, winemaker, and goodwill ambassador—illuminating the lessons of the past and innovating the future of wine. Carlo is the keeper of the stories and the flame.

FAMILY TIME

Why Napa?

My great-grandfather Cesare and great-grandmother Rosa Mondavi set things into motion back in 1919, when Prohibition was voted into law. They owned a small boardinghouse and saloon in Minnesota that was shut down as a result of the Volstead Act. My great-grandfather was charged by the town with the honor and challenge of going to California to search for wine grapes to ship back so the families of the town could make home wine. This was one of the loopholes of Prohibition as the state did not want to go against the church and its sacrament, nor against traditional medicinal uses of alcohol. So they came to California and eventually to Napa Valley.

After Prohibition was repealed in 1933, my great-grandparents bought a little winery with the money they'd saved and began making wine. At that point, Napa Valley became my family's home and has remained so for the past four generations. My grandfather Robert and grandmother Marjorie raised my father, Tim, in the same town my brothers, sisters, and I would grow up in. It's also the same town where my father met my mother.

CARLO MONDAVI

the **OENOPHILE**

HAT

T-SHIRT

I got my love of hats from my grandfather. I don't have a crazy collection, but if I'm traveling and see a cool hat, I'll grab it. A hat needs to have a story, and most of my mine do.

BOOTS

CARLO'S
Daily Uniform

DENIM

Carlo's
**GOOD-TIMES →
CAR**

Something about Napa just makes me want to drive a drop-top vintage car. My favorite is a 1974 Toyota Land Cruiser or a 1964 Lincoln Continental.

CARLO'S FAVORITES

WHAT IS YOUR FAVORITE WEEKEND EXCURSION, ACTIVITY, OR RITUAL?

I love the Sonoma Coast. I grew up surfing out there—it is so pure, clean, and untouched.

Favorite
SECRET PAIRING

"A glass of Cabernet with breakfast on Sunday. I rarely do this, if ever, but once I caught my grandfather having steak, eggs, and Cabernet and thought it was the coolest thing ever. It reminds me of him and also is just damn good."

STEAK & EGGS

+

CABERNET

Q&A with Carlo

YOUR FAVORITE RESTAURANT? Thomas Keller is a Napa Valley treasure. What he has done for food not just here but in the culinary world inspires me. I love his restaurants and his bakery.

YOUR FAVORITE WINERY? Scribe reminds me of what you might have seen at Robert Mondavi back in 1966 before corporate America started second-guessing intuition. It's a couple of young brothers, Adam and Andrew, following their dream in wine and having fun doing what they love. The property and team all have great energy.

IF YOU COULD GET A RESERVATION ON A MOMENT'S NOTICE IN NAPA, WHERE WOULD IT BE? Ad Hoc's fried chicken Mondays-any day of the week.

WHAT IS THE BEST-KEPT SECRET? The snacks at Meadowood from Chef Kostow.

YOUR FAVORITE WATERING HOLE? Pancha's for a dive bar and Cadet for amazing wine.

YOUR FAVORITE BEVERAGE GLASS? I love traditional Burgundy stems for most all wines ... even Champagne.

YOUR GO-TO HOUSE WINE? I love Burgundy and Pinot Noirs from New World producers that have restraint. The Sonoma Coast and Santa Barbara are producing wines that are blowing my mind in the Pinot camp ... Littorai, Hirsch, Domaine de la Côte, Cobb, Scribe, Lola. I also drink a fair amount of RAEN, which my brother and I make.

the FAMILY BUSINESS

From left: Tim, Chiara, Carlo, and Carissa Mondavi, and friends

"ALWAYS GET BACK UP."

Great things have come from the darkest of times for my family. Prohibition put us out of business; then when it was repealed in 1933, it put us out of business again. In 1943, my grandfather persuaded his parents to purchase Charles Krug Winery in Napa Valley, and in 1965, he was kicked out—leading to the start of Robert Mondavi Winery in 1966, then Opus One in 1979. We never wanted or intended to sell the family business, but new laws came about in 2001, and shortly after, in 2004, we lost Robert Mondavi Winery, Opus One, and everything. Things happen; it's awful, sad, and frustrating, but when you fall down, you must get back up. Always get back up. Now, standing where we are, it seems like a blessing. We have Continuum. My brother Dante and I started RAEN Winery and life is not just good, it is great. I still get emotional about what happened when I think about it, but I'm very proud of what my grandfather and father have been able to accomplish. As my grandfather would say time and time again, even in his nineties, "It is just the beginning."

CARLO MONDAVI

CONTINUUM: THE LEGACY CONTINUES

Continuum was founded in 2005 by my grandfather Robert; my father, Tim; and my aunt Marcia and is my family's legacy and our everything. Back in 1966, my grandfather's goal was to prove that we could make wines that could sit among the world's finest. People laughed at him, but he knew after visiting with the first growths of Bordeaux and grand crus of Burgundy that we had the soil, climate, and know-how to make wines capable of reaching those heights; we just needed to invest in our vineyards and cellar. Fifty years later, here we are with several of the finest houses in Bordeaux, owning properties in Napa Valley, and all of that achieved with the notion of my grandfather being crazy. Don't get me wrong—there is a level of crazy to his dreams, but it is the right kind of crazy.

Carlo and his father, Tim

"Sounds cliché, but if you are in Napa Valley, make it a point to visit a family-owned winery. The reason so many people started coming to Napa Valley remains the one thing you should not miss."

the FAMILY BUSINESS

Carlo and Dante (far right)

WHY RAEN?

RAEN is my and my brother Dante's Pinot Noir project way out on the far hills of the Sonoma Coast. A big source of inspiration for us has been the Pinot Noirs my father made in the 1970s and 1980s, along with some of our friends' wines that are being made way out there. The landscape, air, and life out on Sonoma Coast is simply incredible, and when all the choices in a season are made properly, these areas can yield some of the best wines.

The name RAEN comes from a story my father would tell us. He would say that rain naturally turns to wine if you do nothing at all. Rain falls on the fields and filters through the rocks; then the vine drinks and the sun sweetens it while on the outside of a grape, there is a wax that collects the native yeast and microflora floating through the air. A bird might peck the grape, or gravity would bring it to the ground, and the berry would crack open and the sweet juice would mix with the yeast on the skins. Sugar plus yeast yields alcohol, and right then and there, without us touching a thing, rain would turn to wine. So it's a play on words . . . RAEN standing for the purity of rainwater to wine.

CARLO MONDAVI

WHAT DID YOU WANT TO DO OR BE AS A CHILD?

I knew I wanted to become a winemaker and do what my grandfather and father did from a very young age. I was not quite sure what that meant, but they had so much love for wine and all that it encompasses . . . I just knew I wanted to do what they did and work with them.

WHO WAS YOUR WINEMAKING INSPIRATION?

My grandfather and father have both been and continue to be my greatest inspirations in wine and in life. I still stand outside the winery on the phone with my father for long conversations, and the lessons my grandfather taught me hold true now more than ever. Even when life is hard, I have to remind myself how lucky I have been to have those two as my teachers.

CARLO'S
Go-To Gift

CARLO WITH HIS GRANDFATHER, ROBERT MONDAVI

WINE OPENERS

WINE TASTING 101

The best part of wine is enjoying it with a meal where the wine elevates the meal and the food elevates the wine. With that said, I love tasting wine in all sorts of settings, and I basically approach wine with the same three steps whether I'm in the cellar, blinding wines, or just out and about. Sight, smell, swirl, taste, and repeat. All of these steps reveal so much about where the wine comes from, what the variety is, how it was farmed, when it was picked, how it was fermented and aged, and if the wine was stored properly.

1

SIGHT

Sight shows you so much—from the core of the wine or center deepest part of the wine, all the way to the rim. The core shows you how deep, dark, and intense the color is, which does not necessarily translate to intensity of wine as logic might lead you. However, sight does reveal if the wine is thin-skinned like Pinot Noir or thick-skinned like Cabernet. The wine, as it brushes up on the glass, leaves tears and stains the glass. This all gives you an idea of viscosity, which also reveals notable signs about the wine and its possible origin and vinification.

2 SMELL

Smelling the wine opens up the world of winemaking, possible country of origin, and should help you confirm any initial thoughts you might have had on sight.

3 SWIRL

When a wine is first poured, I typically swirl after smelling because sometimes there are initial delicate notes when poured that swirling might blow off or change. Remember, the wine is alive and will continually open as you give it air and time. Taking notes and going through these steps when just enjoying or blinding wines has been helpful for me.

4 TASTE

Taste gives you another layer with flavor, revealing tannin, acid, structure, weight, and notes about the wine, to layer over what you smelled and observed.

Introducing

AGUSTIN FRANCISCO HUNEEUS JR.

THE SUPERSTAR

Agustin Francisco Huneeus Jr. is a Chilean-born marketing superstar—an amazing combination of both industry insider and outsider, with a serious eye and nose for *big* success. His street cred is his visionary breakthrough with the category-defining wine brand The Prisoner, which sold in 2016 for a record-breaking industry price. Agustin Francisco has spent the last thirty years working alongside his father, Agustin Huneeus Sr., overseeing some of Napa Valley's most successful wine ventures, such as Quintessa, Faust, and Flowers.

→
NAPA VALLEY WINE AUCTION

the BUSINESS

INSIDER OR OUTSIDER?

Both. Growing up, I wasn't a Napa insider, but I was constantly exposed to the wine business throughout my childhood, when my father was working at Seagram Chateau & Estates. He always took me on trips to the important wine regions in the world, and when my dad went out to dinner, I would stay at iconic places like the Brolio Castle in Italy and Châteaux Lafite in Bordeaux. It was quite an education. By the time I was twelve, I had been to most of the great wine-growing regions and many great wineries. In that sense, I consider myself an outsider to Napa, but an insider to the wine industry.

FIRST JOB IN THE WINE BUSINESS?

My first job was in the export department at Concha y Toro, but in no way did I see wine as my calling. It was 1988. I was just out of college. I couldn't get a job anywhere else. And I wanted to live in Chile and immerse myself in that side of my heritage. It was a great experience, but I actually couldn't wait to get out of the wine business. I applied to business school, and my first real career was as an investment banker. It was only later that I really came to appreciate all that the wine industry had to offer.

YOUR DAD WAS IN THE WINE BUSINESS. HOW DID HE INFLUENCE YOU?

My father came to wine through more of the viticultural perspective, which allowed me to focus more on the sales and marketing. We've complemented each other very well in that regard. I got started in the industry in 1995, and it was through my father. I was working in investment banking and he was running Estancia and Franciscan in Napa, and he had just lost his head of sales and marketing. I loved my career, but working with my father was an opportunity I didn't want to pass up. Not because it was the wine industry, per se, but because it was a chance to work with my dad. I didn't want to let that opportunity slip by and look back later with any regrets. It was a good decision. My father and I have been working together for more than thirty years now. To this day, there is nobody I call more frequently with questions and thoughts. His perspective has always had an enormous influence on me.

WHAT ABOUT THE PRISONER?

I grew up in a wine industry governed by a lot of dogma. Certain wines had to come from certain places, so that if you were going to make a red blend, it had to be Cabernet and Merlot. What I loved about The Prisoner was that it didn't follow the rules. Everything about it was unique. The label. The blend. There was nothing about its provenance that would have made you think of it as fine wine. But it was brilliant wine. And I saw how people reacted to it. I remember when I was first getting into the wine industry and Merlot was starting to happen, my dad reminded me that there was supposed to be a little pain in fine wine, that it was supposed to hurt a bit, like good coffee. But The Prisoner took a shortcut to the pleasure senses. At the same time, our company already had traditional wineries such as Flowers, Faust, and Quintessa. I was attracted to the fact that The Prisoner was younger, hipper, cooler.

AGUSTIN FRANCISCO HUNEEUS JR.

the OENOPHILE

THE PRISONER, A CROWD FAVORITE

AGUSTIN WITH HIS WIFE, MACA

HOW DID THE PRISONER VISION COME TO LIFE?

Our approach was entirely grassroots and word of mouth. We took the opposite tack of the big wine brands. We wanted there to be scarcity. We gave customers allocations. We treated it as an allocated wine.

WHAT MADE THE PRISONER SUCH A MONSTER SUCCESS?

Everything I touched on above. The wine style, and the fact that it was very high quality but broke all the rules. It was innovative but also relevant. And it was a good value. That, too, is a crucial point.

WHAT'S THE NEXT EVOLUTION IN THE WINE WORLD?

The wine world is going to continue to evolve toward fine wine, with the United States leading the way in innovation, driven by Napa. We're going to see a lot of exciting developments in the years to come.

HOW WOULD YOU DESCRIBE HOW THE WINE INDUSTRY HAS EVOLVED?

When I got into the wine business in the mid-nineties, you could have bought land in Napa for $10,000 to $15,000 an acre. Today, the price is closer to half a million to three-quarters of a million dollars, so there's that. But from our perspective, the other big change is that in the nineties, it was all about big brands. Mondavi, Kendall-Jackson, Estancia, names of that sort of scale and renown. For years, the wine business was like a big animal, and the fine wine business was just a freckle on it. Times have changed. We're living in a world where people care intensely about the quality and provenance of their food. And that now applies to wine as well. Fine wine is booming. But we're only at the beginning of that boom.

HOW WOULD YOUR FATHER DESCRIBE HOW THE BUSINESS HAS EVOLVED?

I think he would agree with the evolution as I've traced it. But he also thinks of the wine business in terms of categories, as in, say, Napa Cabernet being a strong category. He would say some categories are doing great, while others are still emerging. So not all fine wine is doing just as well. California is doing better than many other places. But of course he recognizes that more and more people are drinking wine every day and it is more and more a part of American culture every day. He would agree that we have made a lot of progress.

WHERE DO YOU SEE THE WINE BUSINESS HEADING?

I expect the fine wine business to continue to grow, especially as Millennials increasingly get into wine. When I was growing up, young people didn't drink wine. It wasn't part of the lexicon or the landscape. Things are very different now. I've always said that when we sell wine, we aren't just selling liquid in a bottle. We're selling everything around it—the pedigree of the fruit, the story of the production, the lifestyle attached to it. That's more relevant today than ever. When I bought The Prisoner, it was a small brand, and in just five years, we grew it into one of the most popular wine brands in the world. That was one of the signals of where the industry was heading, and I expect it to continue. The fine wine business will continue to grow, and we will see other powerful high-end wine brands emerge.

Q&A with Agustin

WHAT IS YOUR FAVORITE GUILTY WINE PLEASURE WHEN NO ONE IS
LOOKING?
My favorite wine pleasure isn't a guilty one. It's pairing
a good white Burgundy with crab that, quite simply, hits
it out of the park.

WHAT IS YOUR GO-TO HOUSE WINE?

When you're in the business, you drink your friends' wine.
I'm lucky to have a number of good friends who make wonderful
wine. Those are what I keep in my cellar.

YOUR FAVORITE RESTAURANT?
For a splurge, The French Laundry. I also love dining on the
terrace at Auberge du Soleil, which has wonderful, simple,
seasonal food and some of the most spectacular views in the
valley. I love Redd Wood, Richard Reddington's place in
Yountville.

IF YOU HAVE FRIENDS IN TOWN, WHAT'S THE ONE THING NOT TO BE
MISSED?
A picnic in a Napa vineyard or at a park. Or, maybe better yet,
a visit to the pavilions at Quintessa, which my wife designed.
Instead of tasting in a winery, you get to taste in the context
of a vineyard. It's a unique and wonderful experience.

← PARENTS, VALERIA & AGUSTIN

→ AGUSTIN WITH HIS FATHER, AGUSTIN SR.

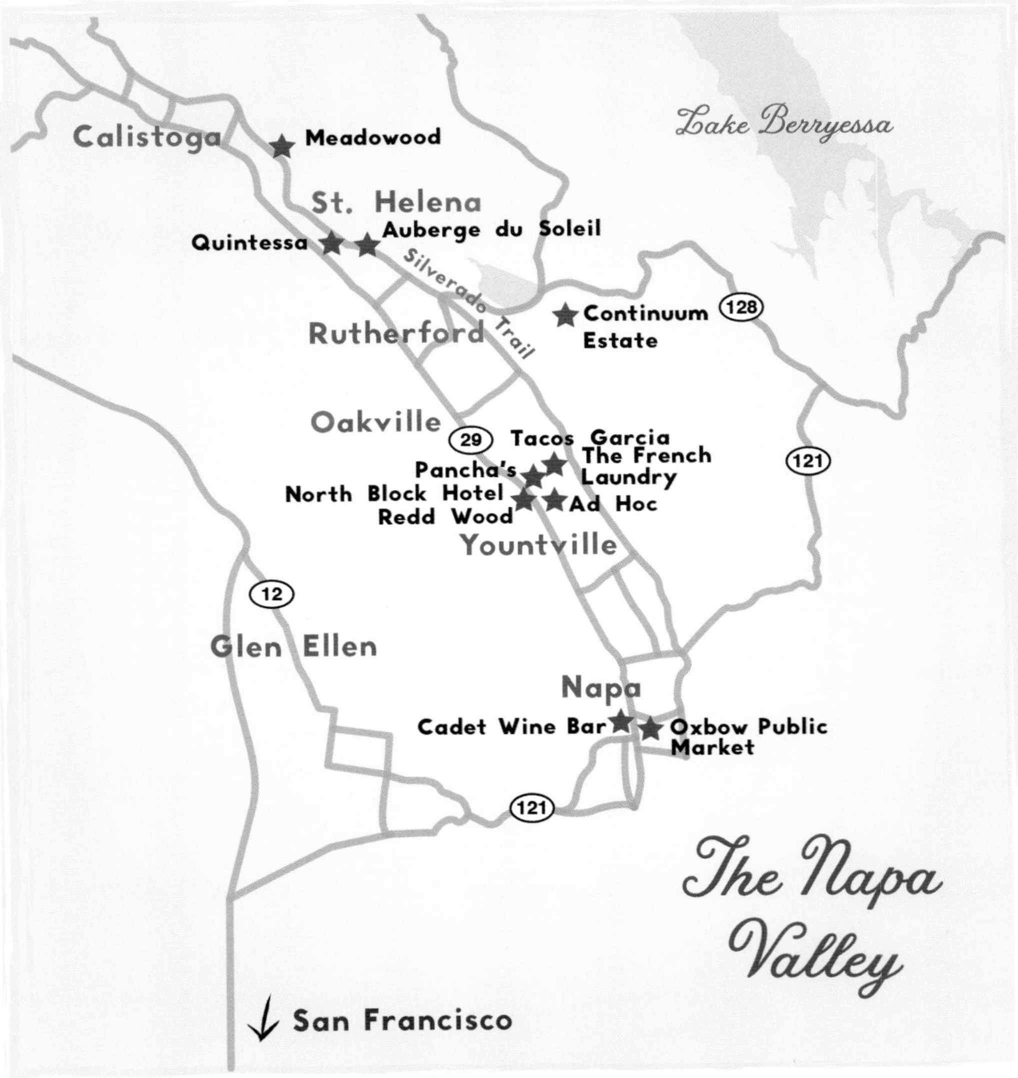

Calistoga

★ Meadowood

St. Helena

Quintessa ★ ★ Auberge du Soleil

Silverado Trail

Rutherford

★ Continuum Estate

(128)

(121)

Oakville

(29) ★ Tacos Garcia
Pancha's ★★ The French Laundry
North Block Hotel ★★ ★ Ad Hoc
Redd Wood

Yountville

(12)

Glen Ellen

Napa

Cadet Wine Bar ★ ★ Oxbow Public Market

(121)

↓ San Francisco

Lake Berryessa

The Napa Valley

Alexis's

OENOPHILE
GUIDE

WHERE TO STAY
WHERE TO EAT
WHERE TO WINE

LODGING: NORTH BLOCK HOTEL

In the self-proclaimed culinary capital of Napa Valley, Yountville, the boutique North Block Hotel quietly sits at the north end of Washington Street in understated glamour. Its Tuscan-style façade gives visitors to wine country a little taste of the charming Italian countryside. All twenty rooms have heated bathroom floors, soaking tubs, and separate rain showers as well as king-size beds. It's the perfect little oasis for the out-of-towner or the staycationer who wants pure, posh luxury.

Though it's a tiny property, it plays host to an upscale restaurant, Redd Wood by James Beard–nominated chef-owner Richard Reddington of famed Redd restaurant. Redd Wood is a pizza joint that churns out wood-fired pizzas and homemade pastas in a chic but unfussy environment.

North Block Hotel
6757 Washington Street
Yountville, CA 94599
northblockhotel.com

EATERY: TACOS GARCIA

Tacos Garcia
Pancha's Parking Lot
6764 Washington Street
Yountville, CA 94599

In the parking lot of dive bar Pancha's in posh Yountville, the unofficial culinary capital of Napa Valley, sits a food truck—a taco truck, to be exact—serving some of the most delicious and authentic Mexican fare. All walks of life seem to congregate with one another in the serpentine line during the lunchtime hour: Tesla-driving tourists; viticulturists and winemakers; locals; Yountville workers. And what brings them together is the joy of the taco.

Arguably the most inexpensive yet delicious meal you can have in the valley, Tacos Garcia's extensive menu offerings range from a mini taco at $1.75 a pop to beef tongue, burritos, or taco salad for $10. And better still is that it's fast food—food that doesn't require you to sit inside or tip for the speedy and tasty service. The truck used to be a well-kept secret, but not anymore. The secret is out and everyone wants a taste.

WINERY: CADET WINE & BEER BAR

The owners of Cadet Wine & Beer Bar say that the wine and beer list are pro-California, but I'd go so far as to say that Cadet is pro-experimentation. First, let's talk about the name: Colleen Fleming and Aubrey Bailey wanted to hearken back to the original meaning of the word, which means trainee, and with that, the ethos of Cadet Wine & Beer is to teach people how to navigate the world of wine in a way that isn't intimidating. A noble goal. The offerings span the globe, bringing a distilled list of some of the best wine and beer producers into one place.

The sleek forty-nine-seat wine bar has a sultry, homey feel, no doubt created by the low lighting and candles, chalkboard menu, communal tables in rich woods, and intimate setting. To add even more of a loungey vibe, Cadet owns a variety (read: *tons*) of LPs that guests can choose from to narrate the soundtrack of their lives. Sometimes there's nothing better than a glass of wine, some tunes, and friends.

**Cadet Wine &
Beer Bar**
930 Franklin Street
Napa, CA 94559
cadetbeerandwinebar.com

167

MICHAEL BAUER'S

PERFECT DAY IN NAPA

Most people travel up and down the valley to various wine-tasting rooms. However, my suggestion is to park your car and spend the day in downtown Napa.

That would have been a pretty boring proposition a decade ago, but now there's enough to fill a weekend. You'll find about two dozen winery tasting rooms within walking distance. You can weave in and out of them as you head to the next culinary destination on my agenda.

Any time you want to drop out you can always head to the Napa River Inn spa in the historic hotel, or to one of the other spas in the downtown area.

MORNING:

10 A.M.: Start the day at **Oxbow Public Market**, a forty-thousand-square-foot space just across the river from downtown Napa, featuring artisan foods and wines. Enjoy some **Blue Bottle** coffee and a cinnamon morning bun at **Model Bakery**. Don't have two cups, however. Head to **Ritual,** another local roaster, and compare. Then meander around the businesses: **Hog Island Oyster Company**, the **Wine Merchant**, and many others.

11:30 A.M.: Head to **Angele**, a charming French restaurant located in a converted boathouse. Sit on the covered patio overlooking the Napa river and have the warm country pâté. Of course, you could have a full-on lunch but there's plenty more to see and taste.

BEST COFFEE IN TOWN

AFTERNOON:

12:30 P.M.: Stop by **Zuzu** (weekdays), a Spanish tapas restaurant, for such items as the braised pork cheeks with black radish salad and fresh Gulf shrimp with garlic, chili, and paprika.

2 P.M.: Drop in to the **Bounty Hunter**, a retail wine store and restaurant with an impressive inventory. Order the beer can chicken, which comes to the table gloriously bronzed and standing straight up on a beer can. It's some of the best roast chicken you'll find.

4 P.M.: For a mid-day pick-me-up, stop by **Napa Valley Coffee Roasting Company** on Main Street for a cappuccino.

EVENING:

6 P.M.: Head to **Oenotri**, which is known for Southern Italian specialties. I'd have a pizza and maybe one or two of the house-made charcuteries. Of course there's always cocktails and wine, too.

8 P.M.: **Miminashi** is a Japanese izakaya that not only has a stunning interior, but equally fully-realized food. You may think you're full but you won't be able to pass up the yakatori, which is made from every part of the chicken. Plus, there's a great sake list and some of the best cocktails in the valley.

10 P.M.: Finish up your evening at the **Cadet Wine & Beer Bar** which is owned by Colleen Fleming (of Kelly Fleming Wines) and Aubrey Bailey, former French Laundry sommelier. It's a favorite local hangout and a great place to try something you've probably never tasted before.

THE OXBOW PUBLIC MARKET

The Oxbow Public Market in downtown Napa is a true foodie emporium. Today, it is packed on the weekends with locals and thrill-seekers looking to taste, try, and swoon. And much like the Ferry Building in San Francisco, it is becoming the hub of the emerging Napa community and a must-visit destination for the gastronomically inclined and out-of- town visitors. And behind it is the Model Bakery and the Fatted Calf. The possibilities are endlessly delicious.

SOME OF MICHAEL'S FAVORITES

Drakes Bay Oysters, Hog Island Oysters
Wet cappuccino, Ritual Roast
Salmon tacos, C Casa
Chocolate cupcakes, Kara's Cupcakes
Milk coffee ice cream, Three Twins
English muffins, Model Bakery
Cheeseburger, Gott's
Juice bar, Hudson Greens and Goods
Charcuterie, Fatted Calf

ROMAN COPPOLA

Introducing

THE TASTEMAKER
ROMAN COPPOLA

with

HOWARD BACKEN
and
VERONICA SWANSON BEARD

ROMAN COPPOLA

Roman Coppola is one of the great storytellers today—possessing a tender heart, exquisite imagination, droll humor, and a deep appreciation for the nuances of life. These traits have helped him win a Golden Globe for Best Television Series for *Mozart in the Jungle* and an Academy Award nomination for Best Original Screenplay for *Moonrise Kingdom*, with cowriter Wes Anderson. Everything about Roman Coppola could inspire a story—from his tortoiseshell indoor-outdoor prescription sunglasses, last seen on Ari Onassis; to the refurbished, deep indigo Greyhound adventure bus parked under a tree at his Napa home; to his impromptu tailgate picnics complete with hot tea and homemade gingersnaps. Roman is thoughtful, casual, nostalgic, and yet modern. Like his mother, Ellie; father, Francis; and sister, Sofia, Roman came into this world with a tremendous gift of inspiring people to experience another world, another time, and someone else's journey.

PERSOL GLASSES

LACOSTE SHIRT

ROMAN'S *Daily Uniform*

VANS

BERMUDA SHORTS

Why Napa?

I grew up in San Francisco for the most part, and my family thought it would be nice for the kids if we had a weekend home in the Napa Valley. My parents came across what had been the Gustave Niebaum Estate, and it was much grander than they had imagined for a weekend home. They bid on it on a whim—but did not win the auction. A few months later it became available again, and it was too extraordinary to pass up. Once we were lucky enough to become the new owners, my parents realized that this was a place for our family to live permanently. We moved here when I was about twelve.

HOW DOES/DID NAPA INSPIRE YOU AS A STORYTELLER?

There are a lot of characters growing up in the valley—friends from school who had a knack for spinning yarns—not unlike some of the tales you might hear from characters in a Steinbeck novel such as *Tortilla Flat*. There was a particular kind of appreciation for ironic and playful stories that was part of the neighborhood banter—and this has been an inspiration.

ROMAN COPPOLA

WHAT ABOUT NAPA DO YOU LOVE?

I love the weather—it's just perfect. In the summer it gets just hot enough, and in the fall and winter it's just cool enough. Also, being in a winemaking area, there's something sensual about the smells and colors of the changing seasons.

Roman's
GOOD-TIMES CAR ➞

VINTAGE SCHOOL BUS

FAMILY TIME

HOW WOULD YOU DESCRIBE GROWING UP IN NAPA?

Living in the country had its quirks, such as not having television reception. (We loaned a Betamax to a friend, who would tape *Saturday Night Live* and *Monty Python* for us.) So many memories are connected to being outdoors—I had a dirt bike and loved exploring the mountainside on it. Thanksgiving is quite magical. Going out into the vineyard and picking mustard greens is one of those enchanting things . . .

WHAT WERE YOUR CHILDHOOD TRADITIONS AND RITUALS?

Traditions growing up tended to be seasonal: We have a beautiful small lake in the back of our home, and spending time there in summer has always been a highlight. We've also enjoyed tooling around in the unusual cars my dad has, such as his Tuckers or his 1913 Model T Ford. I have a lot of fond memories of trying to start the cars and get them to Calistoga (without overheating) for the Fourth of July parade.

A FOURTH OF JULY NECESSITY

↓

WHAT WAS YOUR PARENTS' PHILOSOPHY ABOUT RAISING CHILDREN?

I grew up in a family that emphasized the arts. My grandfather was a composer and conductor, and all of his brothers were very musical—and that is a tradition that we've kept. We've always valued creativity—my mom is an artist and was inventive with the ways that she raised us, such as entertaining us with drawing games if we were bored in a restaurant. Art was always a big part of growing up in my family. My dad has always been very passionate in his work, and following him on his various projects has been a huge part of my rearing.

**HOME-COOKED
MEALS ARE
A BIG DEAL**

←

WHO COOKED, AND WHEN WERE THE COVETED MEALS?

Growing up in our family, dinner was a big deal, and we would all gather and be present for it. Often, interesting artists and filmmakers would pass through, and impromptu dinners would occur on a moment's notice. My dad would lead the way as the chef, cooking and improvising, with everyone pitching in. When it was just our immediate family, we would eat in our kitchen, while with bigger groups, we would eat in our dining room, but always rather informally.

WHAT IS YOUR FAVORITE NAPA FESTIVITY?

The Fourth of July parade in Calistoga is something I try not to miss. They have a fun carnival at the fairgrounds, often with the sprint car racing, which I have always enjoyed.

WHAT ABOUT NAPA BRINGS YOUR FAMILY TOGETHER?

It's our home. We always gather for Christmas, Easter, and summer, and we especially look forward to these times now that my sister and I have small children—and so the cousins can all run around. Small rituals like picking wild blackberries in the summer, gathering eggs from the chickens, or making lemonade from our tremendous lemon tree are the things that we all enjoy.

HOW OFTEN DO YOU COME OUT TO NAPA?

I come out almost every weekend when I'm in San Francisco, which is where I live. I like to settle in and stay for several weeks (if not months) during the summertime. I am always here Easter and Christmas.

WHAT'S IN YOUR GARAGE?

I have a few: a Honda Pioneer, a little quad four-wheeler that is really fun to zip around the small trails on, and it's able to go up steep hills and through muddy creeks. My kids and I will pile in there and go exploring. When I want to go into town to buy some groceries or go to Steve's Hardware, I'll take my beat-up 1964 Corvette that was a prop used in *The Outsiders*, and it's fun because it's like a ranch car. Then I also have a 1947 Silversides, which is an old Greyhound bus that has been converted into an RV, and I love to take it down to Gott's Roadside or Geyserville to visit our winery there.

"I'm not a snob about drinking wine—I like drinking wine without rules. I don't buy the white wine only with chicken or fish or red wine with red meat. I feel like you should have whatever you want, when the mood strikes you. Once in a while, I'll add a splash of soda water or ice to a glass of red wine on an afternoon. I like being informal with wine and not fussy."

WHEN DID YOU FIRST START DRINKING WINE?

Wine was always present on the dinner table, and we weren't discouraged or particularly encouraged to drink it; it was just there in more of the European tradition. I remember drinking white wine in Paris with lunch when I was twelve or thirteen and first feeling its effects, which was memorable. As a young man of about twenty, I really began to enjoy it in a more meaningful way.

WHAT WAS YOUR FIRST JOB AT THE WINERY?

I remember being encouraged by my parents to pick grapes for a day, and I don't think I lasted more than a few cases' worth. Now I enjoy going out to pick with my children, and each year we make our own batch of about fifteen cases of home wine for our personal enjoyment. More recently I've been participating by guiding our estate Syrah, RC Reserve, which I enjoy crafting under the winemaker's guidance.

HOW MUCH INVOLVEMENT IN YOUR WINES DO YOU HAVE?

I had always enjoyed Syrah, particularly in the style of the Shiraz made in Australia. We had a small amount growing on our property, and I got involved so I would have custom wine for my fortieth birthday. After that, we continued and offered it to the public. I chose the bottle and designed the label and packaging. More importantly, I work with the winemaker to craft the wine in a style that appeals to me. Now whenever a child in the family is born, we make a large-format bottle with their name engraved on it for them to have when they celebrate a significant birthday or a marriage.

Q&A with Roman

YOUR FAVORITE RESTAURANT? There are a few: I love Ciccio because I love the atmosphere and the food is great. I love getting a Negroni and the spaghetti cacio e pepe. I love Gott's Roadside with a big group: my sister and her kids and all of our cousins, in particular.

YOUR FAVORITE WATERING HOLE? I have to say it's Pancha's in Yountville because it's a fun bar more on the divey side, very neighborhood-y, and you can smoke in there, which is rare for a bar these days.

IF YOU COULD GET A RESERVATION ON A MOMENT'S NOTICE IN NAPA, WHERE WOULD IT BE? Ciccio, because they don't take reservations for small parties.

YOUR FAVORITE SHOP? I very much enjoy going into Steve's Hardware, which has wonderful housewares as well. Definitely the Napa Valley Olive Oil Manufacturing Company, which has beautiful cheeses and Italian import goods, from the Particelli family, who are great old family friends. It's one of the first places I remember visiting when we moved here.

IF YOU HAD FRIENDS IN TOWN, WHAT IS THE ONE THING NOT TO BE MISSED WHILE IN NAPA? I would say my favorite thing is just to take friends on an adventure on the back of our property, zipping up the backcountry road, looking out over the beautiful views, and maybe bringing a picnic. Then, second choice would be to pile into my bus and go to Gott's Roadside (ordering ahead, naturally).

ROMAN'S LIMON-MARCELLO RECIPE
named after my son, Marcello

1

X 15

Peel the lemon skins—being careful not to get any of the white (pithy) part.

2

Combine lemon peels with 750 ml of Everclear, or highest-proof grain alcohol.

3

Let maturate for 4 to 6 weeks.

4

Make some simple syrup by dissolving 3 cups of sugar with 3 cups of almost-boiling water.

← **SERVE WELL CHILLED!**

Limon– Marcello

5 Remove the lemon peels from the alcohol. (Some people say to strain it with fine cheesecloth, but I don't bother.) Combine the room-temperature sugar syrup and the lemon peel-flavored alcohol. Mix well. Allow it to sit for a week or so.

HOWARD BACKEN

the

ARBITER OF STYLE

Napa Valley Reserve

Local superstar architect Howard Backen's unique and instantly recognizable style has helped define the Napa Valley architectural vernacular and has become synonymous with high taste, elegance, and spacious comfort. Known for his sophisticated "modern rustic" approach that combines architectural correctness with agrarian utility, Howard's influential design has captured the imagination of tastemakers and architectural enthusiasts, as well as provided the signature look for Restoration Hardware showrooms across the country.

Why Napa?

Living here provides an amazing lifestyle, and people are so friendly and happy to be here. I stay friends with the people I work with long after the project is completed. And I always say Napa is one of the purest places—because of agricultural zoning, you just don't get the big-box stores up here. Once you pass Napa proper and drive farther north, you realize that there is no disintegration on the outskirts and that each vista and building is visually beautiful, and you don't see a lot that doesn't please your eyes. You are in the countryside, but with world-class food, wine, and culture around almost every corner.

Harlan Estate

Meadowood Spa

HOW DO YOU START A DESIGN?

Hand-drawing is as essential and important as the computer in design. I draw inspiration from the site by drawing on the site. The act of siting is as important as the design of the building—indeed, the two are part of the same process. Of course, the placement of a building involves studying a site's geology, wind patterns, sun loads, view corridors, and possible connections to outdoor space; siting also means expressing the axial relationship between a building and its landscape. The directional line is essential.

WHAT IS YOUR DESIGN MOTTO?

I am always looking at ways to connect indoor and outdoor space in simple and compelling ways.

My own house is based upon a simple farmhouse—and farmhouses can vary. It's a series of small buildings, which make up these different environments on the same property. The main house has one main room—not counting the more private bedrooms—with multiple exposures based on the views, which are spectacular. It happens to be all white, inside and out, to balance the light. Light and air are major parts of what I think makes a space most livable.

I bought a building with the intention of using the back half to house my St. Helena office, and I needed to come up with a good use for the front half to make it interesting so I opened a restaurant. Dining and architecture are so physically connected up here, so it made sense. I'm very pleased that it's the kind of restaurant you can walk into during the day or late at night and be equally comfortable.

HOWARD BACKEN

HOW WOULD YOU DESCRIBE YOUR ARCHITECTURAL STYLE?

Well, I prefer not to dwell too much on the idea of style because it's trendy. Style changes, like fashion. I prefer to base my work upon where it is, and in Napa Valley there are so many different landscapes, from hillsides to the valley floor. The style of architecture should, in a perfect world, respect and reflect the landscape and the homeowners. I always say you design a house or a structure based on what is given, and what's given is a lot of things: the budget, the location, the neighbors, the site's orientation to the sun rising and setting. It's as much about what you don't do as what you do. Yet, having said all that, if I were given the freedom to design in any style I wanted, I tend to prefer simple, rustic structures with a strong connection to everything beyond the building.

WHAT IS YOUR FAVORITE BUILDING IN NAPA?

Charles Krug Winery, which was originally built in 1874. In 2012, I redesigned it and the project was completed just in time for Peter Mondavi Sr.'s ninety-ninth birthday in 2013.

Archetype Restaurant

Screaming Eagle

Introducing
VERONICA SWANSON BEARD
THE FASHION STAR

Veronica is my fantastically talented middle sister and is also my best friend, along with our little sister, Claiborne. Each of us found our creative passions early in life: mine was wine; Claiborne's was photography; and Veronica's was fashion. Veronica came into the world with a third eye—as a young girl, she was always observing people and personal expression in any form, but particularly fashion.

Since I can remember, Veronica has walked a razor's edge of being cool and chic. She has always nailed the right choice, look, response, advice, and gut instinct. One day, after years of dreaming and scheming, she announced very matter-of-factly, "I am launching a line of jackets in February." Just like that.

HAT

BLAZER

VERONICA'S
Daily Uniform

DENIM

BLOUSE

DESCRIBE THE FASHION ETHOS OF YOUR LINE.

Veronica Beard is the answer to a wardrobe that rides the line between cool and classic. We design your uniform—the pieces you rely on every day to look and feel your best. Personal style is exactly that: personal. Style is all about the nuances; I always roll up my sleeves and pop my collar on my jacket. I leave one side or the back of my shirt or blouse untucked on purpose. There are no two VB customers who wear the same thing the same way, and that's the only way we would want it.

HOW WOULD YOU DESCRIBE YOUR FASHION JOURNEY?

In high school I became an obsessive vintage shopper and spent every dime I had at church thrift shops, county flea markets, and vintage stores on Haight Street in San Francisco. Hunting for the perfect item became a sport. I was obsessed with vintage bell-bottom Levis, both the jeans and cords, and I couldn't get enough. Vintage T-shirts were a favorite because they were perfectly worn in, as well as vintage leather bags, which had been loved in all the right ways. I still *love* vintage shopping; the more history and love a piece has had, the better. On my last trip to San Francisco I found the perfect vintage Christian Dior fringe Western jacket—it was a vintage shopping miracle!

My adolescent years were spent cycling through three phases: bohemian girl, surfer girl, and preppy girl. I lived for magazines. I am still obsessed with inspiration and mood boards because they remind me of my childhood bedroom walls, which were covered in curated collections of magazine tear sheets. *Vogue* was "it," and fashion was all I cared about.

WHAT DO YOU THINK NAPA VALLEY STYLE IS?

Napa's style is a little bohemian/gentleman farmer, and is effortless and naturally chic.

WHAT WAS THE SPARK THAT INSPIRED VERONICA BEARD?

There really wasn't one thing, although the jacket/dickey concept was the first thing we designed. The concept of the uniform was something that I had always been obsessed with. The women in my life who had a distinct uniform were always the chicest/most interesting to me. The jacket is our signature piece and still our number-one seller.

WHAT INSPIRES YOU?

My kids, and remembering myself as a little girl wanting to do exactly what I'm doing today.

WHAT TO PACK

ARMY JACKET

STATEMENT EARRINGS

PEASANT BLOUSE

 FOR SUMMER

PERFECTLY WORN JEAN SHORTS

SKINNY WHITE JEANS

STRAW BAG

LEOPARD MULES

EASY DRESS

HAT

BOOTIES

FUR VEST

FOR AUTUMN

**TAILORED
BLOUSE**

**LEATHER
TOTE**

CLASSIC TRENCH

**HIGH-WAISTED
JEANS**

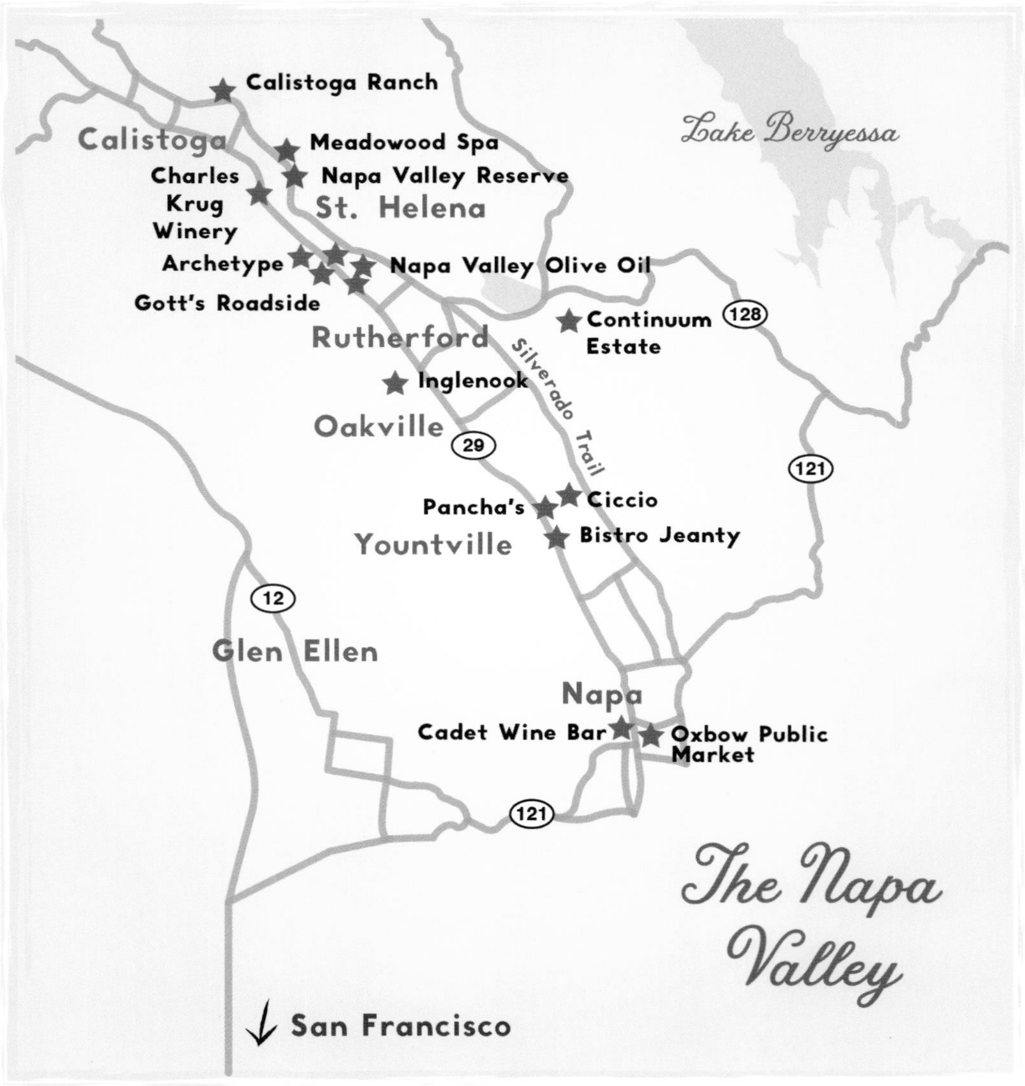

Calistoga Ranch

Calistoga

Meadowood Spa
Napa Valley Reserve

Charles
Krug
Winery

St. Helena

Archetype

Napa Valley Olive Oil

Gott's Roadside

Rutherford

Continuum
Estate

128

Inglenook

Oakville

29

Silverado Trail

121

Pancha's

Ciccio

Yountville

Bistro Jeanty

12

Glen Ellen

Napa

Cadet Wine Bar

Oxbow Public
Market

121

Lake Berryessa

The Napa
Valley

↓ San Francisco

Alexis's
TASTEMAKER
GUIDE

WHERE TO STAY
WHERE TO EAT
WHERE TO WINE
and
MUSTN'T MISS

LODGING: CALISTOGA RANCH

Two words describe Calistoga Ranch: quiet luxury. Nestled among the oak trees in the hills of Calistoga, Calistoga Ranch is the perfect getaway for an über-romantic holiday, girls' weekend, solo retreat, etc. Since it's in Calistoga, it already feels like a world away from everything, but that feeling is further enhanced by the seclusion of the resort oasis, which is composed of forty-nine freestanding, rustic cedar lodges scattered among the hillside. So if you're looking to go incognito, this would be the place to do it. The beautiful, natural environs provide a great setting for indoor-outdoor living that is so pervasive at Calistoga Ranch: on-deck pools and poolside chairs, open-air living and dining spaces, floor-to-ceiling glass doors that lead to more outdoor sitting areas, and trees that grow through the living room floor. It truly is a one-of-a-kind place, with unadulterated luxury at every turn.

↑

**YOUR OWN
PRIVATE NAPA**

Calistoga Ranch
580 Lommel Road
Calistoga, CA 94515
calistogaranch.aubergeresorts.com

Wherever I am, talking with people who have visited the valley in the past two decades, I am always struck by what is embedded in their memory of their trip. There is always talk of Thomas Keller, Gott's, Dean & DeLuca, and Philippe Jeanty's tomato soup. It is an amazing phenomenon that this one dish creates such an indelible Napa Valley association.

Even after all these years, this soup is simply breathtaking . . . it *is* heaven in a puff pastry and the ultimate comfort food, especially during the fall. If the presentation alone doesn't enchant you, the first bite is an explosion of textures and tastes, and promises to slay.

Charming and utterly French, Bistro Jeanty is not ever to be missed.

Bistro Jeanty
6510 Washington Street
Yountville, CA 94599
bistrojeanty.com

Bistro Jeanty Tomato Soup Recipe
serves 6

½ cup butter, unsalted
½ lb. yellow onions, sliced
6 garlic cloves
1 bay leaf
½ tbl. whole black peppercorns
1 tsp. dried thyme leaves
¼ cup tomato paste
2 ½ ib. tomatoes, ripe, cored, and quartered
1 cup water (no more; use only if tomatoes are not ripe and juicy)
4 cups heavy cream
2 to 4 tbl. butter
Salt to taste
½ tsp. ground white pepper
1 lb. puff pastry, or store-bought sheets
1 egg, beaten with 1 tbl. of water

Melt the butter in a large stockpot over medium-low heat. Add the onions, garlic, thyme, bay leaf, and peppercorns; cover and cook for about 5 minutes. Do not let the onions color. Add the tomato paste and lightly "toast" it to cook out the raw flavor. Add the tomatoes and water, if needed. Simmer over low heat for 30 to 40 minutes, until the tomatoes and onions are very soft and broken down. Puree by passing through a food mill, blender, or handheld immersion blender, then strain. Return the soup to the pot. Add the cream, salt, and white pepper, and remaining butter to taste. Bring the soup to a simmer, then remove from heat. Allow the soup to cool for two hours or overnight in the refrigerator.

Divide the soup among six 8-ounce soup cups or bowls. Roll out the puff pastry to ¼ inch. Cut into 6 rounds slightly larger than your cups. Paint the dough with the egg wash and place the circles, egg wash side down, over the tops of the cups, pulling lightly on the sides to make the dough somewhat tight like a drum. Try not to allow the dough to touch the soup. These may be made up to 24 hours in advance and covered with plastic in the refrigerator.

Preheat oven to 450°F. Lightly paint the tops of the dough rounds with egg wash without pushing the dough down. Bake for 10 to 15 minutes, until the dough is golden brown. Do not open the oven in the first several minutes of cooking as the dough may fall. Serve immediately.

WINERY: LORENZA ROSÉ

Everything awesome about summer can be linked back to a glass of rosé. Poolside lunch? Lazy evening porch swing? Bare feet on fresh-cut grass? Rosé goes with all of those, which is why they sip it like water in the South of France during the summer, where contentment wafts through the air like the scent of strawberries and wild herbs. Lorenza Rosé, produced by Michele Ouellet, Napa Valley native and fashion model, and her mother Melinda Kearney, is a tastemaker favorite for its fresh, effortless yumminess that goes with just about everything you can imagine.

Lorenza Rosé
lorenzawine.com

THE WINE
that goes with everything

**Napa Valley Olive Oil
Manufacturing Company**
835 Charter Oak Avenue
St. Helena, CA 94574

While in St. Helena, you want to check out the Napa Valley Olive Oil Manufacturing Company. Established in 1962, this enchanting discovery delights anyone looking for the real deal. The Particelli family runs this old-fashioned Italian market out of a little whitewashed barn, seconds from town, and sell an amazing selection of olive oils, sausages, and olives. Gourmands flock to stock up on their Napa Valley Olive Oil bottles in every imaginable size—the perfect Napa trophy/souvenir.

Introducing

THE HIGH ROLLER

ANN COLGIN

with

TREVOR TRAINA

and

LAURIE ARONS

ANN COLGIN

Every industry has its "Girl Boss," and in the wine business, it would certainly be Ann Colgin, proprietress of cult favorite Colgin Cellars. Having run Sotheby's West Coast Wine Department, where she procured and auctioned the most coveted wines for private wine cellars, Ann has spent her professional life delicately straddling the rarefied auction world and the big leagues of Napa Valley. With her taste and knowledge, she is able to bring patrons, enthusiasts, oenophiles, and philanthropists together over bottles of category-defining wine. In a twist of perfect coincidence, she and her husband/business partner, Joe Wender, reside at Tychson Hill in a restored clapboard farmhouse that once belonged to Josephine Tychson, the first woman to build a winery in the Napa Valley in the nineteenth century. Boom.

LAYERED TOPS

DIAMOND EARRINGS

ANN'S *Daily Uniform* →

FANCY SNEAKERS

LEATHER LEGGINGS

Ann's **GOOD-TIMES CAR**
DARK RED MERCEDES CLS63 AMG →

I drove the car at the *Robb Report* Car of the Year event a few years ago and still love it. It holds those curves and rumbles.

"I love being in a business

that brings people together

over a bottle of wine."

Why Napa?

I attended my first Napa Valley wine auction in 1988 and fell in love with the community. I was already captivated by the wines and loved the beauty of the area, but it was discovering the generosity of the people and the diversity of the land that made me want to spend more time here and produce wine.

I had started my career in the art, antiques, and auction world, and Napa Valley was a perfect retreat. While running the Sotheby's West Coast Wine Department, I met my husband, Joe, at an Henri Jayer wine dinner at Spago in Beverly Hills. He was a collector and connoisseur of European wines, and happily, he fell in love with Napa Valley, too. We got married at IX Estate, the site of our vineyard and winery overlooking Lake Hennessey, in 2000. IX Estate is named for our parcel number on the hill and our wedding date of 9/9. The extremely rocky land had just been prepped for planting, and it had taken one year and lots of effort to remove the rocks. I arrived on a John Deere D9 earthmoving machine for my wedding!

For more than twenty-five years, I have led a talented team that strives to produce exceptional red wines from distinctive hillside vineyards. I love being in a business that brings people together over a bottle of wine.

Q&A with Ann

YOUR FAVORITE HOTEL?

Meadowood, as I think it exemplifies country elegance and luxury.
I also love that it is adjacent to the Napa Valley Reserve, which
is the most amazing and fun club for wine lovers.

YOUR FAVORITE RESTAURANT

Ad Hoc. You can't beat the yummy family-style comfort food. Every
dish is always delicious, especially the fried chicken!

YOUR FAVORITE WINE PURVEYOR

V Wine Cellar is my favorite wine purveyor in Napa Valley.

YOUR FAVORITE WEEKEND PLEASURE

I love hiking around Lake Hennessey. Just be sure to wear sunscreen
and watch out for rattlesnakes when it is hot and sunny.

YOUR FAVORITE WATERING HOLE?

The bar at Press for a great margarita. Having grown up in Texas,
I need that fix every now and then.

HIGH-ROLLER RESTAURANT?

The French Laundry is my favorite special-occasion restaurant.
I love the creative and delicious vegetarian menu, which showcases
the bounty of Napa Valley, but I always reach over to my husband's
plate for a few bites of the fabulous Snake River Farms beef, which
goes perfectly with Napa Valley Cabernet.

HERE DO YOU TAKE OUT-OF-TOWN FRIENDS?

Drinks on the patio at Auberge du Soleil overlooking Napa Valley.

YOUR FAVORITE SIGNATURE GIFT?

The substantial and informative book *Napa Valley Then & Now*,
by Kelli White.

ANN COLGIN

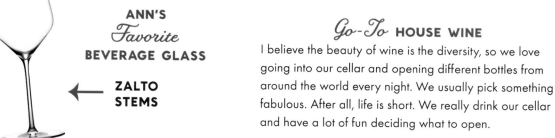

POPCORN + **SHAVED TRUFFIES** + **KONGSGAARD CHARDONNAY**

ANN'S
Favorite
SECRET PAIRING

ANN'S
Favorite
BEVERAGE GLASS

← **ZALTO STEMS**

Go-To HOUSE WINE

I believe the beauty of wine is the diversity, so we love going into our cellar and opening different bottles from around the world every night. We usually pick something fabulous. After all, life is short. We really drink our cellar and have a lot of fun deciding what to open.

ANN & JOE'S UNRIVALED CELLAR

PARTY RITUALS

1 **SPLIT UP COUPLES**

We love to entertain at the farmhouse, where we always split up couples and try to invite someone new to each dinner party. We also serve at least one course of wine blind so that everyone has to guess. I love it when a Francophile is sure the Napa Cabernet is from Bordeaux. We have made some converts!

2 **CONDUCT A BLIND TASTING**

BLIND TASTING 101

I am a big fan of blind tastings because you have to think and analyze the wines. Joe and I do this with friends and clients at dinners, often giving clues to stimulate the conversation. A clue might be "same grape, same year" and the wines could be a California Cab and a Bordeaux. We also taste blind when blending the Colgin wines. Our winemaking team puts together bagged bottles marked "A," "B," "C," etc., and we all analyze the wines and discuss our favorites. We do this periodically throughout the year before deciding on our final blends for each of our wines.

ANN COLGIN

I love opening large-format bottles and having all the guests sign the empty bottles. They are great keepsakes of fabulously fun evenings. Joe and I started the tradition when we were married and had the guests sign a Salmanazar (9L) instead of a guest book. That bottle is still in our wine cellar and brings back such wonderful memories.

3 PARTY TRICK: SIGN THE BOTTLE!

GET WRITING! →

NAPA CLASSICS *with* PAUL ROBERTS & ANN COLGIN

Paul Roberts is a Master Sommelier and has had an illustrious career in the Napa Valley. Today, he works with Ann Colgin at Colgin Cellars. Between Paul and Ann, I knew I was in good hands when I asked them:

WHAT ARE THE QUINTESSENTIAL WINES THAT HAVE DEFINED NAPA VALLEY TO DATE?

PAUL SAYS: Napa Valley has produced world-class wines for over one hundred years. These wineries are some of the stalwart producers that helped to firmly establish Napa in the pantheon of wine-growing regions.

ANN SAYS: These classic Napa Valley wines showcase the depth and diversity of the region. From crisp, age-worthy Chardonnays to beautifully balanced and distinctive Cabernets, the list focuses on vineyards that produce wines of character and personality. When you open the 1974 Heitz Martha's Vineyard you will be transported to an earlier time and you will understand how well Napa Valley wines can age!

WHITE WINES

Stony Hill Chardonnay From the inaugural vintage of 1952, the McCrea family has crafted long-lived Chardonnay from the slopes of Spring Mountain. One of the first wineries to sell directly to private clients. The wines of Stony Hill can easily age for decades. The 1992 and 1994 Chardonnay are amazing today . . . a true testament to this hallowed land.

Smith Madrone Riesling From high on the slopes of Spring Mountain, Stu Smith has crafted a classic Riesling for more than forty years. A wine that combines the pristine fruit of the Napa Valley with the succulence and minerality of the great Rieslings from Europe.

Robert Mondavi I Block Fumé Blanc The oldest Sauvignon Blanc vines in the United States, from vines planted in 1945. The I Block is a section of the famed To Kalon vineyard that produces one of the greatest Sauvignon Blanc wines in the world. This wine ages gracefully for many years. An absolute must-have for the Classics cellar!

RED WINES

Inglenook Cabernet Sauvignon The glorious wines of the 1940s and 1950s produced by John Daniel expressed the heights that red wine could achieve. Extremely rare today, the 1941 is one of the single greatest wines we have ever experienced.

Beaulieu Georges de la Tour Cabernet Sauvignon First produced in 1936, the BV wines of old were the textbook examples of the combination of power and elegance that Rutherford is known for. The wines in the forties and the fifties are legendary, and a statement for the vision of André Tchelistcheff.

Robert Mondavi Reserve Cabernet Sauvignon When Bob Mondavi built his winery in 1966, it was the first new construction of a winery since Prohibition. It served as a catalyst to energize the "new" California wine business. His 1966 and 1978 Reserve wines are beacons of the vision he had for the Napa Valley.

Heitz Martha's Vineyard Cabernet Sauvignon This is one of the first single-vineyard wines produced in the Napa Valley. The famed 1974 stands as legend.

Diamond Creek Cabernet Sauvignon This remarkable estate on the top of Diamond Mountain showed the sheer diversity of the Napa Valley—all in one twenty-two-acre vineyard. Al and Boots Brounstein found that their property showed four distinct geologies, and in turn, four distinct wines. The Diamond Creek wines from the late seventies are a testament to how distinct our soils are—and the amazing diversity of this place. The 1978 Lake bottling is stupendous!

Introducing
TREVOR TRAINA
THE CONNOISSEUR
and the art of
MOTORING IN THE NAPA VALLEY

"For in Napa, the journey is the destination . . . There is something amazing to discover around every corner and there is no hurry. A hidden-gem winery, a delightful picnic spot, a stunning vista all wait to be found. The light, the air, the well-maintained roads all gently coax even the oldest vehicle along with pleasure. As a friend with a car collection put it, there are so many different kinds of wine-country cars. All are welcome."

Trevor Traina is my husband, partner in crime, and favorite playmate—the things he likes, I always like. Trevor has wisely managed to fashion several successful careers around his personal passions: technology, connoisseurship, and cars. The bulk of our weekends are spent tinkering with old cars—some of them working, and some not working—with the hope of a journey somewhere in particular but close to the local towing station. There is nothing in the world I love more than sitting in the passenger seat, going nowhere fast with him.

TREVOR'S
Daily Uniform

PLAID SHIRT

BOOTS

1957 ALFA ROMEO GIULIETTA

JEANS

Trevor's
GOOD-TIMES CAR

TREVOR'S *Favorite* →
SECRET PAIRING

FRENCH DIP AT RUTHERFORD GRILL

+

BIG CAB

ALL IN THE FAMILY: THE LOVE OF OLD CARS

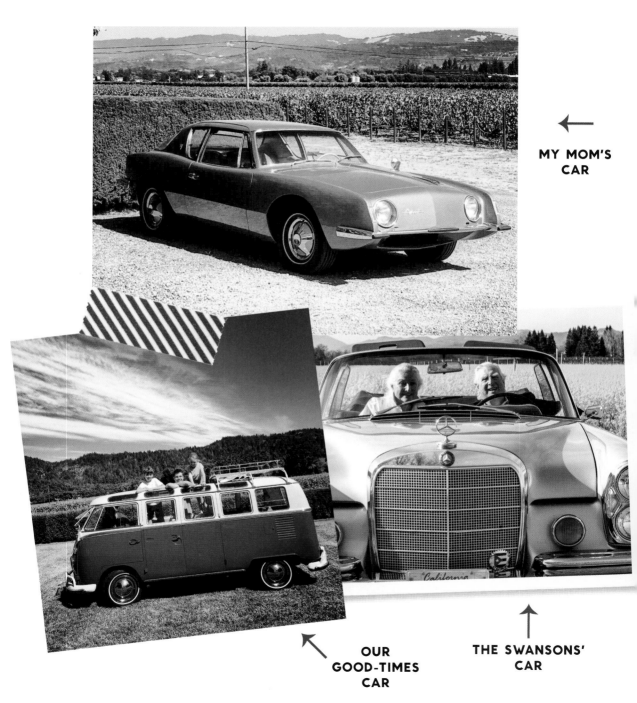

MY MOM'S
CAR

OUR
GOOD-TIMES
CAR

THE SWANSONS'
CAR

↑
**MY BROTHER-IN-LAW
TODD'S CARS** →

Napa and the automobile share a love affair. From the latest TV launch of some new model to the *Robb Report* Car of the Year issue, something subconscious continues to tie vehicles to the meandering roads of the Napa Valley. It is not at all uncommon to see a wonderful vintage truck arranged outside a winery with a welcome sign perched on the windshield. Virtually every serious car collector ships a sports car to the valley at some point. Tourists are equally prone to splurge on the convertible Mustang at the rental counter in the hopes of exploring the back roads with gusto. If you figure in the arrival of NASCAR to the region, the existence of several of America's top car collections, the Legends of Motorsport events at Meadowood, and the beloved Father's Day car show in Yountville, you can't help but notice a pattern.

So why is it that in the valley so famous for wine, driving often trumps drinking? Well, it goes without saying that Napa is a destination reached primarily by car. A bird's-eye view shows that the many well-maintained roads form a ladder of sorts, linking the winery-lined Route 29 ("Highway 29" to the locals) on one side to the panoramic Silverado Trail on the other. Arrayed out from the main arteries are a profusion of meandering lanes that permeate the surrounding mountains and link to the nearby valleys.

This variety represents a treasure trove of options for the motorist. The main highways are superb boulevards for grand touring, admiring the views, and accessing the many incredible restaurants and wineries. And then there are the mountain lanes. Many of them are sparsely used and represent some of the greatest sports-car roads in America.

MY PERSONAL FAVORITES

Our home abuts the Oakville Grade, which soars athletically straight up the Mayacamas Mountains above Harlan and beyond before eventually cresting toward Sonoma. Locals know it is a great road for any high-performance car. I remember as a boy, my father told me about how he had borrowed his father's Mercedes and about racing a Porsche the entire stretch to Napa. I think of him as I drive his 1957 Alfa Romeo Giulietta Spider down the same road, top down, admiring the incredible vistas. An even guiltier pleasure is to wake early and take my Audi R8 up. I start right at Route 29, accelerating past the one-room Anglican church and the To Kalon vineyards until I hit the hill. Paddle shifting the curves, I pass bikers and motorcyclists alike. Up and over, past the hillside fire station and through the one-lane bridge and then up the next set of hills. It is an adrenaline-pumping thrill speeding past moss-laden oaks, taking in the misty, early morning beauty while pushing the car to its limits.

While high-performance vehicles find much to love off the beaten path, there is no real need for speed, as almost every single road in the entire county boasts a superb view or something to recommend. And there is no reason required to motor about. We have no shortage of "vital" errands that require pulling an older car out from the back of the garage.

Another favorite drive with my wife meanders around a small hill past pastures of cows and orderly rows of vineyard punctuated by owl boxes on valley oaks. In the summer the hills undulate from waving golden grasses. In the winter the varied greens of the new vegetation are almost overwhelming. At night, frogs cry loudly from the surrounding creeks. By day, newborn calves hide behind their mothers' legs. It is all right there, but without a car it will never be found.

THE ROUTES

When friends ask me which routes they should take, I tell them there is no wrong way to go and that exploration is half the fun. However, there are a few routes I can recommend. There is no shame at all in simply driving **Highway 29** all the way to **Calistoga**, stopping as much as needed for wine tasting or a perfect meal. Yountville should be accessed via the first exit, and the main street eventually rejoins 29, which continues up through Oakville and Rutherford to briefly become the stunning main street of St. Helena, where it runs by the handsome stone facades and nineteenth-century Masonic buildings before becoming a highway again. For scenic trips, the **Silverado Trail** is also easy and lovely, and the stretch from Big Ranch Road to Calistoga is terrific. For mountain motoring, **Redwood Road** leads up from the town of Napa to the Mayacama Mountains, where it becomes Dry Creek Road. It snakes through evergreen groves and by drop-away views until intersecting the Oakville Grade. Across to the east, **Pope Valley** sits above St. Helena and is another unspoiled area to be discovered. As there are fewer businesses in the neighboring eastern valleys, a picnic or cooler make good sense. I have been lucky to drive them all in one of our many classic cars, and there is no wrong answer.

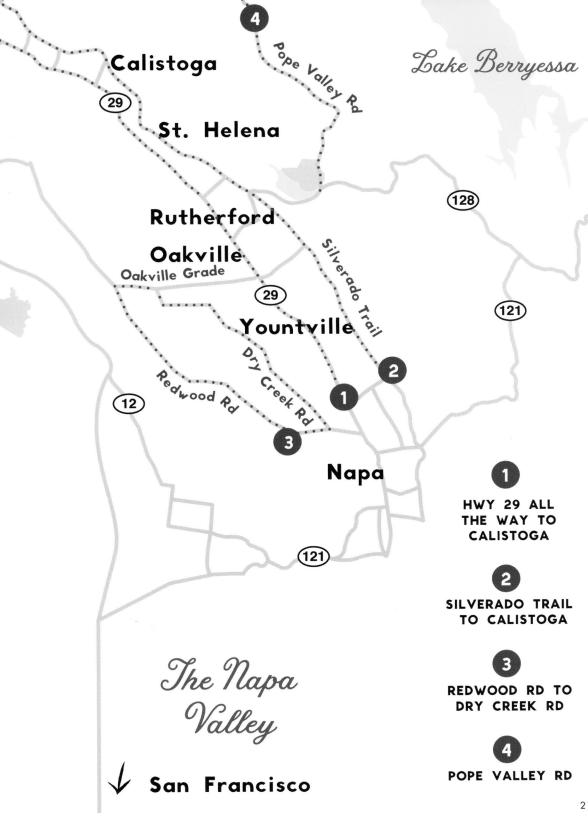

4 Pope Valley Rd

Lake Berryessa

Calistoga

29

St. Helena

128

Rutherford

Oakville

Oakville Grade

Silverado Trail

29

Yountville

121

Dry Creek Rd

Redwood Rd

12

1

2

3

Napa

121

The Napa Valley

↓ San Francisco

1 HWY 29 ALL THE WAY TO CALISTOGA

2 SILVERADO TRAIL TO CALISTOGA

3 REDWOOD RD TO DRY CREEK RD

4 POPE VALLEY RD

FATHER'S DAY IN NAPA VALLEY

One of our family's pleasures has been the Father's Day car show in Yountville. What makes it so charming is that the variety of vehicles on display ranges far and wide. Anything but a testosterone overload, the occasional Ferrari is more than offset by a vintage Buick or a jaunty Model A Ford. Last year we entered two cars, a vintage Fiat Jolly and our 1967 VW Beetle, "Herbie Striped." My brother, Todd, entered our father's old woodie wagon from the 1950s. I remember riding in it on a previous Father's Day with a huge wicker picnic basket secured on the back rack. We had piled the whole family in and driven to one of our vineyards for a spectacular picnic. My father was in heaven until, upon our return, the entire transmission fell out. And yet, even such a calamity was not a big deal in the valley, as we really had nowhere in particular to go, and a good flatbed is never more than fifteen minutes away!

One of the vehicles we entered at the car show, the Fiat, had been a gift for our wedding, and we frequently zip through the vineyards in it, or even over our own lawns and through our hedges, as a Jolly can go almost anywhere!

The Bug is equally beloved and is simple enough that we have been using it to teach our nine-year-old son how to drive a manual transmission. He prefers to ride in the back of my grandfather's 1958 Rolls, though, and loves to put the glass driver partition up and down as I drive the gang to Gott's Roadside for hamburgers.

WE LOVED THESE TWO BEAUTIES FROM THE FATHER'S DAY SHOW

OUR HERBIE & TODD'S WOODIE

←

THE FIAT

WEEKEND ACTIVITY

SERIOUS BUSINESS

Droning around the Napa Valley is a true pleasure. As a verdant ribbon of mostly waist-high plantings, the valley is a perfect place to be casting a drone about. There are few tall trees or unseen obstacles to endanger or ensnare an errant drone, and the views stretch to the hills. Modern drones have lenses better than most top-of-the-line cameras and can capture the nuanced light that defines the stages of a Napa day in such unique ways. From the first gold of dawn to the very deep lavender that precedes the crimson sunsets, a drone at five hundred feet or more registers it all.

→

**HARD TO
BELIEVE
IT'S REAL**

Introducing

LAURIE ARONS

THE WEDDING PLANNER

DETAILS.
DETAILS.
DETAILS.

Laurie Arons is the Bay Area's most sought-after wedding planner, known for incredible destination weddings and celebrations in the Napa Valley. What makes Laurie's work so distinctive is that she provides her clients with some of the most talented vendors and purveyors in celebration magic—caterers, bakers, bartenders, florists, musicians, entertainment, event producers, tent sources. She has seen it, done it, and knows what works.

WHAT MAKES NAPA VALLEY SUCH A DISTINCTIVE DESTINATION?

All of my clients want to have that true Napa Valley vineyard wedding. It feels like you're in one of the faraway wine regions of Tuscany or France, and you're not. You are in the United States and the services are right here, at a very high level. It is an exotic, dreamy destination that happens to be in your backyard. The weather is amazing—there are no bugs or humidity. And of course, the food and wine is always a huge draw.

Napa is more relaxed by nature because it is in the country. Clients are looking for great service yet don't want it super stuffy. The combination of the high standards in a relaxed setting draws people to this area.

IS THERE A FREQUENT THEME?

The multiday wedding. People want to create defining experiences that lovingly reveal who they are, what they love, and what and who is meaningful to them. Thoughtful gestures presented through choice of location, menu, wine pairing, tablescape, entertainment, cake, time of year, time of day. It's the idea of creating and sharing with others memories, friendship, time, and love that cannot be experienced in just one single night.

The multiday wedding is the perfect stage for mixing traditions, combining stories, and honoring cultures.

LAURIE'S WEDDING BLACK BOOK

Favorite
**TOP THREE
NAPA VALLEY
WEDDING VENUES**

1 **Z Modern Estate** has the most spectacular views of the Napa Valley. The property is gracious, expansive, and luxurious.

2 **Meadowood** is wonderfully accommodating, allowing creative license and beautiful tenting.

3 **Black Swan Lake** is like getting married in your own private, spectacular park that comes complete with weeping willows, a lake, and vineyards. It is super manicured, magical, and romantic.

LAURIE'S WEDDING BLACK BOOK

Favorite
CATERER

If you can dream it, **Paula LeDuc** can create it. Her food quality is flawless—it's like eating five-star dining wherever you could possibly imagine.

Favorite
CAKE BAKER

Sam Godfrey is everything. His cakes taste so good—I would be so heavy if I saw him more, because I would be eating them all day long. Cake sets the tone for so much: It's the first thing guests see at a party and the last thing they remember. Sam's cakes taste even better than they look. When you taste them, you close your eyes and you go to heaven, you go to your grandma's kitchen—it's pure magic.

Best

WINE CAVE FOR
SMALL CELEBRATIONS

The most spectacular wine cave is
Hall Rutherford

Favorite

CRAFT COCKTAIL PURVEYORS

Rye on the Road provides an unforgettable craft cocktail experience by combining old-school bartending with modern trade secrets. These truly bespoke mixologists have that hipster vibe, and it's super cool to mix their offerings with a formal wedding.

Best

SMALL PRIVATE DINING ROOM
FOR 10 TO 20 GUESTS

The Brix Cottage is charming and intimate, surrounded by raised garden beds, vineyards, and the train tracks. What's so great about it is that you can make it yours by adding your own personal touches and decor.

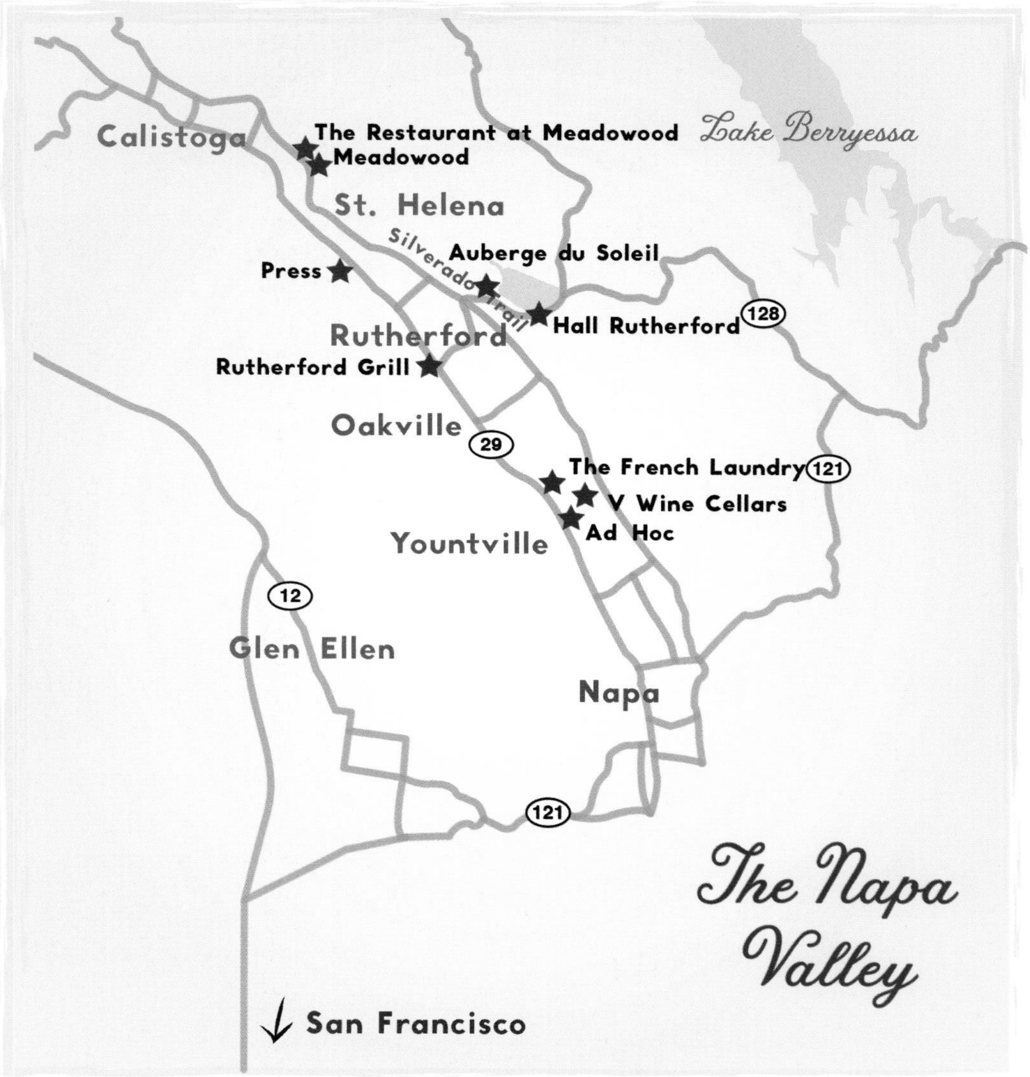

Calistoga

The Restaurant at Meadowood
Meadowood

Lake Berryessa

St. Helena

Silverado Trail

Press ★

Auberge du Soleil

Hall Rutherford (128)

Rutherford

Rutherford Grill ★

Oakville (29)

The French Laundry (121)
V Wine Cellars ★
Ad Hoc ★

Yountville

(12)

Glen Ellen

Napa

(121)

The Napa Valley

↓ San Francisco

Alexis's

HIGH ROLLER
GUIDE

WHERE TO STAY
WHERE TO EAT
WHERE TO WINE
and
MUSTN'T MISS

LODGING: MEADOWOOD

Meadowood
900 Meadowood Lane
St. Helena, CA 94574
meadowood.com

Meadowood is a far cry from its early, simpler days. It is now a Relais & Châteaux property, catering to the bon vivant, foodie, high roller, tastemaker, oenophile, and summer folk with its 250 acres of tennis, nine-hole golfing, hiking, swimming, and croquet. The resort boasts world-class spa facilities, an adult pool and kiddie pool, and, last but not least, a dining room awarded three stars by Michelin and overseen by supertalent Christopher Kostow.

→

**BOOK A
COUPLES
MASSAGE**

The Restaurant at Meadowood
900 Meadowood Lane
St. Helena, CA 94574
therestaurantatmeadowood.com

When you go to The Restaurant at Meadowood, prepare to be in awe. For one, the restaurant itself is just stunning. Resident wine-country architect Howard Backen created an airy space replete with barn-like vaulted ceilings, low lighting, and warm woods to induce the cozy-luxe factor and immediately conjure images of quintessential wine-country dining. It is a restaurant that has won just about every award known to man. The cuisine is certainly what we'd call haute cuisine or high gastronomy, and Chef Christopher Kostow is the inventive genius at the helm. And it's not uncommon to dine for four hours or more, savoring what for some may be a once-in-a-lifetime experience.

ASTON MARTIN   **FERRARI**   **MASERATI**

**TAKE A
SCENIC DRIVE**

The best concierges in the Napa Valley recommend Exotic Car Collection by Enterprise for the best fleet of luxury and exotic cars in Northern California. Exotic Car Collection shared with me their fan-favorite cars for Napa. Any of these and so much more can be yours for twenty-four hours. Rental includes pick up and delivery at any Napa Valley location.

exoticcars.enterprise.com

THE WINERY: OVID

Ovid
255 Long Ranch Road
St. Helena, CA 94574
ovidvineyards.com

Perched at the tippy top of the highest point of the Napa Valley, holding the valley's most magnificent far-reaching views, is Ovid. Expect charming, knowledgeable hosts—occasionally winemakers and principals—in an environment where everyone on the tiny staff overlaps and shares a fierce dedication to meaningful details, ongoing education, and discovery. Visits to the Howard Backen-designed winery are private and by appointment and tend to book a number of months in advance. Total production hovers around one thousand cases in a robust vintage. Claim your spot on the waiting list—it could be awhile.

Introducing

ALEXIS SWANSON TRAINA

the

AUTHORESS

My name is Alexis Swanson Traina. I am a wife, a mother of two young children, and until recently, the creative director at Swanson Vineyards in Rutherford, where I worked with my dad since graduating from college. When I was a child, my family lived in a small town in southwest Florida, where my after-school friends were the elderly ladies of the neighborhood who taught me everything I know about dark chocolate, cards, port wine cheese, housecoats, and men. I credit them with imparting crucial trade skills for later in life.

In my awkward tweener years, I was obsessed with Lady Diana Spencer and insisted on having her same hairdo, eagerly spritzed with several bottles of Sun-In . . . not a good look in a tropical climate for a brunette with braces and poufy hair. By the time I got to boarding school, things had started to come around: I'd found a new hairdo, a new zip code, Benetton, and a whole new set of friends.

And then one day, the pay phone rang in my dormitory. It was my dad calling with life-changing news: "We're moving. We've just bought a vineyard in the Napa Valley." I knew about Napa Valley only from my favorite Friday-night TV show, *Falcon Crest*, which deliciously chronicled the lives of the Gioberti/Channing family and a gorgeous, lazy playboy named Lance Cumson, played by Lorenzo Lamas.

As we hung up the phone, I wondered just how far *Falcon Crest* and Lorenzo Lamas were from this new vineyard. Life was definitely looking *up*.

UMMMMM, YEAH

LORENZO

SEEING MY FUTURE AT THE DORMITORY PAY PHONE

Why Napa?

In 1985, my serial-entrepreneur father, Clarke Swanson, was in-between businesses and on the prowl for something very new and different. Acting on a real estate tip from a fraternity brother living in the Napa Valley, my dad purchased a hundred acres on the Oakville Cross Road, relocated his family, hired the godfather of American winemaking, André Tchelistcheff, and his young apprentice, Marco Cappelli, and began making wine under the label Swanson. My beloved mother, Elizabeth, preferred the simple pleasures of Snickers and Coke, but promised to bring her A-game and New Orleanian charms. It is fair to say that the Oakville Cross Road has never been the same—and neither have we.

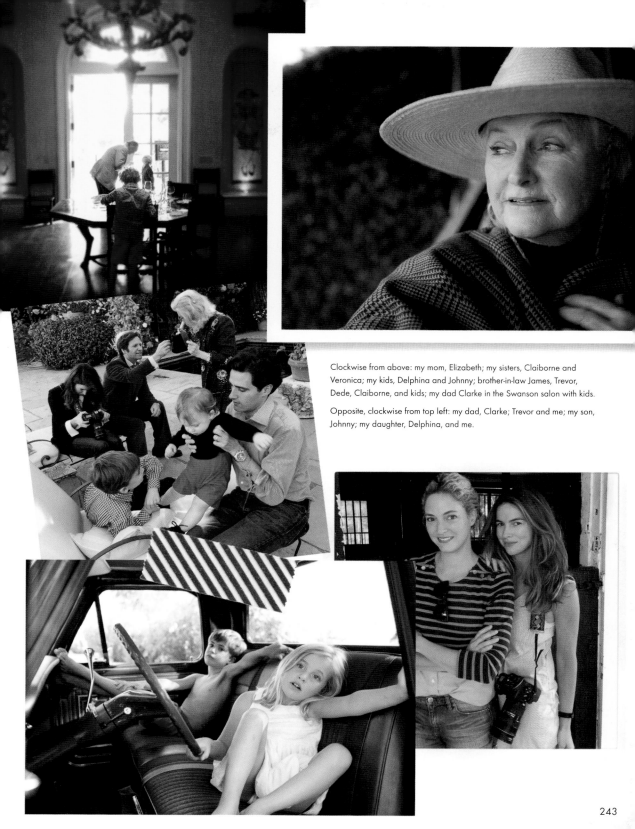

Clockwise from above: my mom, Elizabeth; my sisters, Claiborne and Veronica; my kids, Delphina and Johnny; brother-in-law James, Trevor, Dede, Claiborne, and kids; my dad Clarke in the Swanson salon with kids.

Opposite, clockwise from top left: my dad, Clarke; Trevor and me; my son, Johnny; my daughter, Delphina, and me.

My parents' vineyard on Oakville Cross Road.

OAKVILLE

Clockwise, from top right: my brother-in-law Todd, sister-in-law Katie, and my niece Daisy; Trevor with Johnny and Delphina in Herbie; Dede.

Today, the town of Oakville (population: 300) is a two-mile-wide patch of soil that runs across the valley floor—and is considered to be the most highly valued agricultural land in the United States. Oakville is home to some of the most famous wineries in the world, including cult Cabernet producers Harlan Estate, Screaming Eagle, Opus One, and many wines made from the revered To Kalon vineyards. It is safe to say that Oakville is ably representing America on the international wine stage.

My husband, Trevor, and I, along with our children, Johnny and Delphina, live in San Francisco, but spend our weekends and summers in Trevor's childhood home just down the street from my parents. Together with my brother-in-law Todd, my sister-in-law Katie, and their daughter, Daisy, we live at To Kalon, in the former home of Napa Valley's original wine king, H. W. Crabb—the epicenter of the famed To Kalon Vineyards.

We live at Mr. H. W. Crabb's former home, To Kalon.

"Whoever lives a half a century hence will find the grapes of California in every city of the Union; her raisins supplying the whole Western Hemisphere; her wines in every mart of the globe, and then, with her golden shores, her sunny clime, and vine-clad hills and plains, will California, indeed, be the Vineland of the world."

—H. W. Crabb, 1880
Proprietor of To Kalon Vineyards & Cellars

Coming to CALIFORNIA

After graduating from a small liberal arts college in upstate New York, I moved to California, where my family now lived, and somehow convinced my dad to hire me at his winery. With a straight face and résumé in hand, I told him that I was certain there would be "many other employers" eager for my professional services and unique point of view—but I wanted to offer my talents to him first. Like the blindly devoted father he is, he took the bait and gave me my first real job.

It quickly became obvious that muddy, messy vineyard management wasn't the perfect fit for me—plus there was too much driving around in old, dusty trucks. After I'd worked a few harvests in the cellar, Marco, our winemaker, concluded winemaking wasn't for me either and sweetly convinced me to explore marketing. I quickly discovered that I loved and happened to be good at storytelling, packaging, and creating memorable experiences.

In the summer of 2000, we opened the Swanson Salon in Rutherford—a sensory explosion and laboratory of conviviality. This was a time when the Napa Valley wine-tasting experience was anything but discerning and loaded with lots of inexpensive, belly-up-to-the-bar tasting action, T-shirts, tchotchkes, and thick, clunky wineglasses. I know it is hard to believe, but I swear to God it's true. It was obvious to us that the tasting experience begged for an overhaul, and we were eager to take up the challenge.

We called upon our usual coterie of talented friends and relatives to help us transform an old wine cellar into magic. From there, we brought out our collections of French show tunes, vintage Porthault cocktail napkins, silver candelabras—and served caviar and potato chips with Pinot Grigio; curry-covered Vosges Haut-Chocolat bonbons with our best Oakville Cabernet; stinky blue cheese with sweet, syrupy Late Harvest Semillon; and poured rosé all day long. And we turned up the volume on hospitality and wine education, and catered to both the current and aspiring oenophile. We restricted supply, offering three seated tastings a day, by appointment only. Our plan was deliciously high–low, poetic, and charming. Everything that wasn't yet happening in the valley.

At first, we opened our doors and waited. People in the area were amused by us and this whole "salon" concept. And then suddenly the phone did start to ring—with a flood of eager ladies, calling to book hair and nail appointments while tasting wine. Imagine our surprise day after day, having to explain ourselves and our novel notion of a "salon." But then one day, it took off.

SWANSON
VINEYARDS

SOME OF MY
FAVORITE MOMENTS

↑

ALEXIS
CAB

FOR
THE
PERSON
WHO
HAS
EVERYTHING

THE
SWANSON
SALON

↙

THE SIP SHOPPE:
A CANDY STORE
FOR ADULTS

GLASS DIXIE CUPS

VOSGES HAUT-CHOCOLAT →

→ **CAVIAR**

HELP IS HERE
MODERN HOUSE WINES

WITH LOVE
MODERN HOUSE WINES

EXPENSIVE
MODERN HOUSE WINES

MODERN HOUSE WINES

Ceremonies & **RITUALS**

Over time, it became clear that the ceremonies and rituals of wine had embedded themselves into our daily lives, telling the story of who we were and what we valued. Through wine, we remember specific things: those who gathered together; what we wore; the weather outside; the favorite foods shared; the shape and contents of glasses raised. No memory has more weight than any other. In these particular instances, wine is served as a gesture of appreciation, honor, love—hand chosen to convey the significance of the occasion. Wines themselves became the exclamation point for any occasion, woven into the remembrances of the time and place. Moments like these defined and refined my passion for wine and inspired this book.

Here are some of mine.

OREOS + MERLOT

**DOBERGE CAKE +
SANCERRE**

**CAVIAR + POTATO CHIPS +
SOUR CREAM**

**PORT WINE
CHEESE
+
WHEAT THINS**

I'm One
Drink Away
From Telling
It All

PIMIENTO CHEESE
+
ROSÉ

BBQ CHIPS
+
ROSÉ

OYSTERS +
PINOT GRIGIO

FAVORITE SECRET PAIRINGS...
EVERYBODY'S GOT SOME

As with all things secret, I have discovered that most people have a favorite, naughty go-to wine treat—a type of food-and-wine pairing reserved for behind-closed-doors pleasures, involving comfort and junk foods, not to mention intriguing varietals and surprising wine choices.

MY
Signature Gift

Working on a project at Swanson Vineyards with Andy Spade in 2009, I sensed a strong shift in our evolving wine community. People were eager to express themselves with wine—in what they served, what they brought, and what they gave. Pursuing that intuition, we created "statement-making" Modern House Wine, putting universal sentiments and gestures on good label design—defining moments big and small.

MODERN HOUSE WINES

MY
Personal Love
LANGUAGE
CHOCOLATE

Since the early days of the Salon, pairing chocolates with our fanciest red wines was always a signature pleasure and one that Katrina Markoff (proprietress of Vosges Haut-Chocolat) and I took seriously, with a wink. Katrina and I were eager to break out of the typical cheese-and-crackers rabbit hole and get brazen with our wine pairings at the table. Our first collaboration was the sublimely delicious Alexis Bonbons—naughty morsels of dark chocolate infused with our Alexis wine, and dusted with curry powder and pink peppercorn. Then there were the Trevor Bonbons served at our wedding as table favors—a carefully constructed concoction in honor of the owner of the biggest sweet tooth I know. His recipe included dark chocolate, chicory coffee, and vanilla beans. These bonbons were so sinfully good that we later introduced them as the Petit Morceaux Bonbons. Lastly, for my dad's seventieth birthday, Katrina and I surprised him with a chocolate bar all his own, riffing off the famous Clark Bar. Instead, his bar was called the Clarke's Bark—an old-fashioned chocolate toffee candy bar, fashioned after his favorite childhood candy.

← **NEW YEAR'S DAY**

BABY WINE/BABY CHAMPAGNE

I love that the ceremonies of the dinner table have meaning and purpose. I ask myself, why shouldn't children have precious ceremonies of their own? Charming accoutrements of their own? Generosity of spirit is a learned behavior, and the dinner table is the most fertile ground.

For our family dinners, we serve our children Concord grape juice and sparkling apple juice disguised as "baby wine" and "baby Champagne." Our children even cherry-picked their way through my favorite collection of cordials and identified—with great pride—their own "baby wine glasses." With these miniature goblets, they stand up and make toasts to loved ones around the table, throughout the year.

Some women are crazy about handbags and shoes; I am obsessed with colored cut crystal, aka bohemian glassware—old-fashioned stemware your grandmothers and great-aunts had in their creaky china cabinets. The kind of glassware you see at all the flea markets, swap meets, and antiques shops—everywhere, if you look for it. I collect all kinds of colored cut crystal: I live for them in the small cordial size, served with sweet wine on a porch, at a formally or informally set table, and by the fire, where the flickering light brings their jewel tones alive.

GLASSES, GLASSES &
MORE GLASSES...
everyone HAS A FAVORITE

Favorite
HORS D'OEUVRE
DEVILED EGGS

My deviled eggs are kind of famous—they are online in *Food & Wine*'s Top 10 Deviled Egg Recipes. Not joking.

Deviled eggs are the perfect hors d'oeuvre/snack/lunch/dinner. There are hundreds of sinful ways to prepare deviled eggs, but I am a purist and insist on my eggs made with as few ingredients as possible. I deeply dislike any kind of pickled or fishy contamination in my deviled eggs. I like my eggs bite-size (small to medium), simply dressed with mayonnaise, powdered mustard, a dash of Worcestershire sauce, a drop of Tabasco, and garnished with Maldon salt flakes for a crunchy finish. Now you know.

I LOVE BOUCHON'S DEVILED EGGS, TOO →

Favorite
FOOD GROUP
TOMATOES

During the summer, tomatoes become their own food group, and for two months, they thrive at the tippy top of the Napa Valley food chain. As anyone visiting our house in the summer knows, tomatoes are served round the clock. Tomato lovers know which farmers' markets, roadside stands, farmers, and restaurants carry the most outrageous tomato selection—varieties like Dark Queen, Bleeding Heart, Afternoon Delight, Lucid Gem, Marvel Stripe, Cherokee Purple, Brandywine, Pink Berkeley Tie Dye, and other coveted beauties.

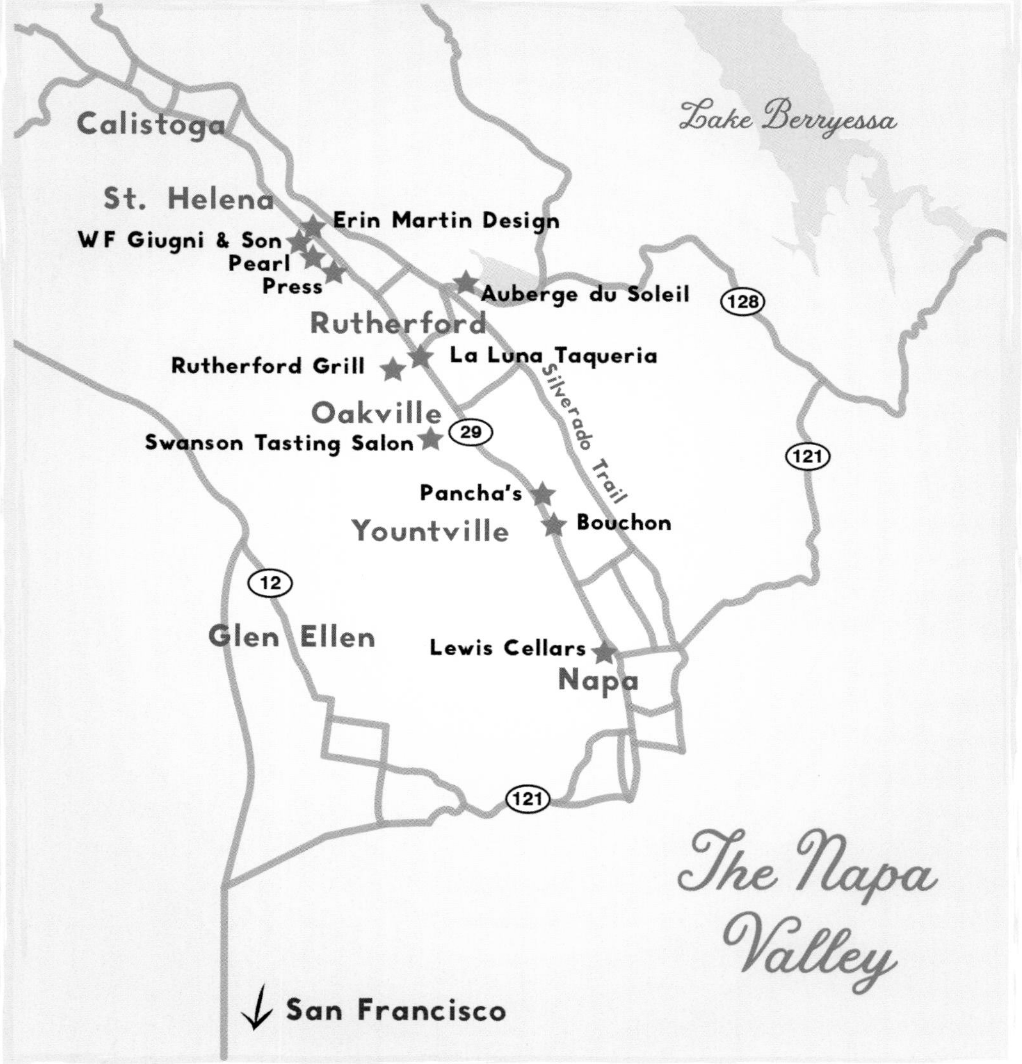

Calistoga

St. Helena

Erin Martin Design

WF Giugni & Son
Pearl
Press

Auberge du Soleil

128

Rutherford

Rutherford Grill   La Luna Taqueria

Oakville

Swanson Tasting Salon   29

121

Pancha's

Yountville   Bouchon

12

Glen Ellen

Lewis Cellars

Napa

121

↓ San Francisco

Lake Berryessa

Silverado Trail

The Napa
Valley

Alexis's

GUIDE

WHERE TO STAY

WHERE TO EAT

WHERE TO WINE

and

MUSTN'T MISS

My FAVORITES ... AND MUSTN'T MISS

LADIES' CLOTHING STORE

Pearl Wonderful Clothing is always a top stop for me, as they carry a well-curated selection of eclectic jewelry, chic straw hats, espadrilles, layering pieces, and a super-stylish brand mix such as Isabel Marant, Figue, Herno, and Ulla Johnson. Best of all, they carry Veronica Beard!

PEARL WONDERFUL CLOTHING

HOME ACCESSORIES STORE

ERIN MARTIN DESIGN

Erin Martin has got style for days. As an interior designer, her fingerprints are all over the place locally, and her latest reveal is Richard Reddington's chic pizzeria, Redd Wood. Vignettes of her world are on display in downtown St. Helena at her showroom, a space loaded with extraordinary and brilliantly edited vintage and contemporary finds that transform rooms in an instant. My favorite section in her shop is her over-the-top collection of photography books. Erin's shop is a destination store that inspires all day long.

RESTAURANT DISH

Calling all bacon lovers: *run*, don't walk, to Press and order up the irresistible bacon tasting. It's a true culinary extravaganza, illuminating the best purveyors of bacon in the land, such as Triple Thick Nueske from Wisconsin; Benton's Country Bacon from Tennessee; Snake River Kurobuta from Idaho; Durham Ranch Wild Boar Bacon from Wyoming, and Hobbs Candied Mangalitsa Bacon from California. Every single bite is a sensory explosion of aroma, taste, texture, chew, smoke, salt, sweet, and heat. You'll find a truly memorable experience that is breakfast, dinner, and dessert all at the same time.

FAMOUS BACON TASTING →

WATERING HOLE

Pancha's is a local treasure, and like nothing you'd ever expect to find in the Napa Valley. In truth, you are more likely to come across something similar in Mexico or along Route 66. The owners run a very authentic establishment, one that is seedy and tragically hip at the same time, with a jukebox, two pool tables, and respectably priced drinks. PS They only take cash!

My FAVORITES ... AND MUSTN'T MISS

World-Famous ENGLISH MUFFINS

The Model Bakery serves Stumptown coffee and espresso, along with the most beautiful iced cookies, small cakes, brownies, and perfect affogatos. Most important, the Model Bakery is world famous for their soft, puffy, and fluffy classic or spelt English muffins, which sell out in a flash.

← **MODEL BAKERY**

What Not to MISS
GIUGNI'S

VINTNER'S DAUGHTER

W F Giugni & Son Grocery is a local darling/institution/obsession that has been around for more than a hundred years, as lore has it. Giugni's is famous for their awesome sandwiches drenched in their ridiculously delicious Giugni Juice, a staple ingredient made up of olive oil, vinegar, herbs de Provence, and roasted garlic that is worth the trip alone! A visit to Giugni's is like a walk down memory lane, with date stamps.

Best DISCOVERY

Created by April Gargiulo, Vintner's Daughter is a crazy-good botanical serum. Made from twenty-two of the world's most active botanicals, it has an international cult following because, truth be told, it gives you the skin you always wished you had. The company Vintner's Daughter was founded in Napa Valley and shares the same commitment to refinement and quality as fine wine producers.

LA LUNA MARKET

La Luna Market & Taqueria on Rutherford Road is an old-school, authentic Mexican market busting out the very best Mexican tacos, quesadillas, burritos, tortas, and nachos in the valley, hands down. They also happen to carry the best selection of real-deal, wide-brimmed straw hats—the kind that all the vineyard farmers use and the kind they don't sell on Amazon.

↑

**THE BEST
STRAW HATS**

La Luna Market
1153 Rutherford Road
Rutherford, CA 94573
lalunamarket.com

LODGING: AUBERGE DU SOLEIL

The Auberge du Soleil, nestled in the terraced hills of Rutherford, is a major splurge and super treat with its intoxicating and heavenly views, fireplaces, pool, spa, wine list, room service, and dining patio. This hotel is the number-one game in town and nothing compares in the winter or summer.

Auberge du Soleil
180 Rutherford Hill Road
Rutherford, CA 94573
aubergeresorts.aubergedusoleil.com

Tip!
**GO TO THE BAR,
GRAB A BURGER &
A BOTTLE OF RED,
AND PLAY SCRABBLE**

EATERY: RUTHERFORD GRILL

In the tiny food mecca of Napa Valley, the Rutherford Grill—a Houston's restaurant—is my favorite, and has an hour-long wait that no one ever seems to care about. There is something deeply nostalgic about the Rutherford Grill: The restaurant is dark and cozy with bloodred leather booths and intoxicating with the smell of sizzle and the noise of shaking ice—all ingredients for a *big time*. Their old-school menu is chock-full of American classics, but their messy, juicy barbecue ribs are to die for as is the French dip sandwich, decadently followed by their epic Oreo ice cream sandwich. Their exceptionally edited wine list carries the very best wines in town made by many of their most regular customers. *Why?* Because every single vintner loves the Grill as much as I do, and it is a badge of honor to have your wines sold there.

My other faves include Bistro Jeanty, Bouchon, and Redd Wood in Yountville.

← WORLD.
CLASS.
RIBS.

Rutherford Grill
180 Rutherford Road
Rutherford, CA 94573
rutherfordgrill.com

Lewis Cellars
4101 Big Ranch Road
Napa, CA 94558
lewiscellars.com

I like big, juicy, slurpy, velvety American wines. Not French, not Italian—not because they aren't great; they are just too elegant and refined for my taste and don't scratch the right itch. I like red wines made by a sophisticated hand using just the right amount of oak, with a generous middle palate and a haunting, lingering finish. To me, Lewis Cellars' red wine program captures the spirit of what Napa Valley wines are all about. Their tasting room in Napa is a no-frills affair, pouring knock-your-socks-off wines. For all the same reasons, I also love all of Kirk Venge's wines, Caymus Vineyards, Macauley, and MacDonald wines.

DIRECTORY

Ad Hoc
6476 Washington Street
Yountville, CA 94599
thomaskeller.com/adhoc

Alpha Omega
1155 Mee Lane
St. Helena, CA 94574
aowinery.com

Andie's Cafe
1042 Freeway Drive
Napa, CA 94558
andiescafenapavalley.com

Angele
540 Main Street
Napa, CA 94559
angelerestaurant.com

Archetype
1429 Main Street
St. Helena, CA 94574
archetypenapa.com

Atelier Fine Foods
6505 Washington Street
Yountville, CA 94599
atelierfinefoods.com

Auberge du Soleil
180 Rutherford Hill Road
Rutherford, CA 94573
aubergeresorts.com

Bardessono
6526 Yount Street
Yountville, CA 94599
Bardessono.com

Bistro Don Giovanni
4110 Howard Lane
Napa, CA 94558
bistrodongiovanni.com

Bistro Jeanty
6510 Washington Street
Yountville, CA 94599
bistrojeanty.com

Bouchon Bakery
6528 Washington Street
Yountville, CA 94599
thomaskeller.com

Bounty Hunter
975 1st Street
Napa, CA 94559
bountyhunterwine.com

Bouchon Restaurant
6534 Washington Street
Yountville, CA 94599
thomaskeller.com

Brix
7377 St Helena Highway
Napa, CA 94558
brix.com

Cadet Wine & Beer Bar
930 Franklin Street
Napa, CA 94559
cadetbeerandwinebar.com

Castello di Amorosa
4045 St Helena Highway
Calistoga, CA 94515
castellodiamorosa.com

Calistoga Inn
1250 Lincoln Avenue
Calistoga, CA 94515
calistogainn.com

Calistoga Ranch
580 Lommel Road
Calistoga, CA 94515
aubergeresorts.com

Ciccio
6770 Washington Street
Yountville, CA 94599
ciccionapavalley.com

Continuum Estate
1677 Sage Canyon Road
St. Helena, CA 94574
continuumestate.com

Cook St. Helena
1310 Main Street
St. Helena, CA 94574

Darioush Winery
4240 Silverado Trail
Napa, CA 94558
darioush.com

Erin Martin Design
1118 Hunt Avenue
St. Helena, CA 94574
erinmartindesign.com

Father's Day Car Show
Town of Yountville

French Laundry
6640 Washington Street
Yountville, CA 94599
thomaskeller.com/tfl

French Laundry Garden
6601–6639 Washington Street
Yountville, CA 94599

Gott's Roadside
644 1st Street
Napa, CA 94559

933 Main Street
St. Helena, CA 94574
gotts.com

Harlan Estate
1010 Main Street
St. Helena, CA 94574
harlanestate.com

Hall Rutherford
56 Auberge Road
Rutherford, CA 94573
hallwines.com

Hotel D'Amici
1673 St Helena Highway
St. Helena, CA 94574

Hotel Yountville
6462 Washington Street
Yountville, CA 94599
hotelyountville.com

In-N-Out Burger
820 Imola Avenue
Napa, CA 94559

Indian Springs
1712 Lincoln Avenue
Calistoga, CA 94515
indianspringscalistoga.com

Inglenook
1991 St Helena Highway
Rutherford, CA 94573
inglenook.com

Ira Yeager Studio
3061 Old Toll Road
Calistoga, CA 94515
irayeager.com

JCB Tasting Salon
6505 Washington Street
Yountville, CA 94599
jcbcollection.com

Kelly's Filling Station
6795 Washington Street
Yountville, CA 94599

La Luna Market & Taqueria
1153 Rutherford Road
Rutherford, CA 94573
lalunamarket.com

Lewis Cellars
4101 Big Ranch Road
Napa, CA 94558
lewiscellars.com

Meadowood Napa Valley
900 Meadowood Lane
St. Helena, CA 94574
meadowood.com

Miminashi
821 Coombs Street
Napa, CA 94559
miminashi.com

Model Bakery
1357 Main Street
St. Helena, CA 94574
themodelbakery.com

Morimoto Napa
610 Main Street
Napa, CA 94559
morimotonapa.com

Mustards Grill
7399 St. Helena Highway
Yountville, CA 94558
mustardsgrill.com

Napa Town & Country Fair
575 3rd Street
Napa, CA 94559

**Napa Valley Coffee
Roasting Company**
948 Main Street
Napa, CA 94559
napavalleycoffee.com

**Napa Valley Olive Oil
Manufacturing Company**
835 Charter Oak Avenue
St Helena, CA 94574

**Napa Valley Performing
Arts Center**
100 California Drive
Yountville, CA 94599

Napa Valley Reserve
1000 Silverado Trail N
St. Helena, CA 94574
thenapavalleyreserve.com

Napa Valley Wine Train
1275 McKinstry Street
Napa, CA 94559
winetrain.com

North Block Hotel
6757 Washington Street
Yountville, CA 94599
northblockhotel.com

Oenotri
1425 1st Street
Napa, CA 94559
oenotri.com

Ovid
255 Long Ranch Road
St. Helena, CA 94574
ovidvineyards.com

Oxbow Public Market
610 & 644 1st Street
Napa, CA 94559
oxbowpublicmarket.com

Pancha's at Yountville
6764 Washington Street
Yountville, CA 94599

Pearl Wonderful Clothing
1219 Main Street C
St. Helena, CA 94574
pearlwonderfulclothing.com

Perfect Endings
776 Technology Way
Napa, CA 94558
perfectendings.com

Press
587 St Helena Highway
St. Helena, CA 94574
pressnapavalley.com

Quintessa
1601 Silverado Trail S
St. Helena, CA 94574
quintessa.com

Raen
1722 S Coast Highway #1
Oceanside, CA 92054
raenwinery.com

Raymond Vineyards
849 Zinfandel Lane
St. Helena, CA 94574
raymondvineyards.com

Redd Wood
6755 Washington Street
Yountville, CA 94599
redd-wood.com

Restaurant at Meadowood
900 Meadowood Lane
St. Helena, CA 94574
therestaurantatmeadowood.com

Rutherford Grill
1180 Rutherford Road
Rutherford, CA 94573
rutherfordgrill.com

Scribe Winery
2100 Denmark Street
Sonoma, CA 95476
scribewinery.com

Solage
755 Silverado Trail N
Calistoga, CA 94515
solage.aubergeresorts.com

Soo Yuan
1354 Lincoln Avenue
Calistoga, CA 94515

Steve's Hardware Inc.
1370 Main Street
St. Helena, CA 94574

Swanson Vineyards
1271 Manley Lane
Rutherford, CA 94573
swansonvineyards.com

Taco's Garcia
Pancha's Parking Lot 6764
Washington Street
Yountville, CA 94599

V Wine Cellar
V Marketplace
6525 Washington Street
Yountville, CA 94599
vwinecellar.com

Vintage Home
1201 Main Street
St. Helena, CA 94574
napavalleyvintagehome.com

W F Giugni & Son Grocery
1227 Main Street
St. Helena, CA 94574

Zuzu
829 Main Street
Napa, CA 94559
zuzunapa.com

THANK YOU, THANK YOU, THANK YOU!

My #1 THANK YOU goes to my extraordinary father, Clarke Swanson, who brought our family out to California and magnificently changed the course of all of our lives. I have loved riding shotgun with you all the way.

Deepest thanks goes to Alyssa Warnock, my amazing creative partner-in-crime and in #beastmode. May we have a lifetime of juicy projects and painful deadlines together.

And to "book whisperer" Jennifer Raiser who inspired me to get my act together and share the Napa Valley I know and love.

And to Mr. Kenneth Fulk—thank you so much for your generous friendship and for kindly introducing me to the loveliest and most talented man in publishing, my editor David Cashion. Triple thank you to David, Annalea, and the team at Abrams for this very special opportunity.

And to Kelsey Duff, my unflappable "production director" and "book boss"—I couldn't have survived without you or your Dropbox skills. And to J'Nai Gaither for all her spot-on research, copy work, and help at a moment's notice. To super-talented Napa Valley photographer Nicole Bruce, who has knocked herself out for me photographing WHO TO KNOW, WHAT TO DO, and WHAT NOT TO MISS for years and years. Your work only gets better! Thank you to Jason Lang whose soulful photo catalogue of Napa, Swanson Vineyards, and my family brought so much richness and texture to my book. Thank you to the Clark Gable of our generation—Douglas Friedman—for sharing your perfect photos with me.

And to Happy Menocal, whose charming illustrations captured the spirit and allure of the Bon Vivant, the Bohemian, the Foodie, the Summer Folk, the Oenophile, the Tastemaker, the High Roller, and me.

Extra thank you to little sis for providing a treasure trove of gorgeous portraits and spending the most delicious twenty-four hours shooting the book's cover with me—as well as the unforgettable SFC!

Extra thank you to everyone in Napa Valley who jumped into my book, not sure of what they were getting themselves into. I am touched by all your kindness.

Lastly, to Delphina, Johnny, and Trevor who endured endless late nights and weekends of book time. Good news: It's OVER!